WALKS AROUND THREE PEAKS

10 WALKS OF 6 MILES OR LESS

Colin Speakman

Dalesman

First published in 2009 by Dalesman
an imprint of
Country Publications Ltd
The Water Mill
Broughton Hall
Skipton
North Yorkshire BD23 3AG

First edition 2009

Text © Colin Speakman 2009
Maps © Gelder Design & Mapping 2009
Illustrations © Christine Isherwood 2009

Cover: Sulber Nick by Colin Raw

ISBN 978-1-85568-261-0

All rights reserved. This book must not be circulated in any form of binding or cover other
than that in which it is published and without similar condition of this being imposed on
the subsequent purchaser. No part of this publication may be reproduced, stored on a
retrieval system or transmitted in any form, or by any means, electronic, mechanical,
photocopying, recording or otherwise, without either prior permission in writing from
the publisher or a licence permitting restricted copying. In the United Kingdom such
licences are issued by the Copyright Licensing Agency, 90 Tottenham Court Road,
London, W1P 9HE. The right of Colin Speakman to be identified as author of this
work has been asserted in accordance with Copyright Designs and Patents Acts 1988.

Printed by Amadeus Press

PUBLISHER'S NOTE

The information given in this book has been provided in good faith and is intended only
as a general guide. Whilst all reasonable efforts have been made to ensure that details
were correct at the time of publication, the author and Country Publications Ltd cannot
accept any responsibility for inaccuracies. It is the responsibility of individuals undertaking
outdoor activities to approach the activity with caution and, especially if inexperienced,
to do so under appropriate supervision. The activity described in this book is strenuous
and individuals should ensure that they are suitably fit before embarking upon it. They
should carry the appropriate equipment and maps, be properly clothed and have adequate
footwear. They should also take note of weather conditions and forecasts, and leave notice
of their intended route and estimated time of return.

Contents

Introduction

Yorkshire's celebrated Three Peaks offer some of the most spectacular mountain walking in the North of England. Ingleborough, Whernside and Penyghent are rightly regarded as icons of the Yorkshire Dales and have attracted generations of walkers, climbers, potholers and lovers of great scenery. For many years Ingleborough was believed to be England's highest mountain, even though its relatively modest 2,373 feet (724 m) is capped by its near neighbour Whernside, and further north Cross Fell.

You hardly need a guide to these popular routes to the main peaks — just follow the crowds along well-worn trails. There's also the practical difficulty of keeping walks under six miles (9.5 km) in countryside which by its very nature offers long, more strenuous hiking. Only Penyghent can be satisfactorily climbed in less than a six-mile circuit and that walk is over-familiar to most people. This book is about alternative walks exploring less heavily used but equally rewarding parts of the Three Peaks.

So the ten walks in this book deliberately do not go to the well-trodden summits, but focus on slightly less familiar ways in what is still truly Three Peaks Country, dominated as the walks are by the magnificent outline of the three mountains. Ironically, you can sometimes enjoy views of a mountain better close to it rather than actually on it, and one of the delights of walking in Three Peaks Country is the unusual, often dramatic views of the hills themselves from different angles.

All walks are accessible by public transport, by the celebrated Settle-Carlisle railway line or linking local bus services, including the excellent summer weekend Dalesbus network (details at www.dalesbus.org). Whilst all are less than six miles, by the nature of the terrain there are inevitably some steep and strenuous sections, including many ladder-stiles which need agility. It is also important to treat even the foothills of the Three Peaks with respect in terms of having good walking boots, rainwear, drink, warm clothing and a decent map.

All but two of the walks are fully covered by OS Explorer OL2 Southern and Western Dales, but walks 2 and 6 require a short section of OL41 Forest of Bowland to complete. Grid references are also used in the text at points where route-finding can be a shade tricky.

Cleatop Wood

Distance: 5 miles (8 km)
Time: 2¹/₂ hours
Terrain: tracks, field and woodland paths; one steep section
Start: Settle Market Place, grid ref 820637   Map: OS OL2
Parking: choice of car parks in Settle town centre
Refreshments/facilities: inns, cafés and toilets in Settle
Public transport: Settle-Carlisle line from Leeds or Skipton (daily);
bus 580 from Skipton (not Sundays)

This walk to and through a beautiful native woodland and a local nature reserve offers fine views across upper Ribblesdale to the Forest of Bowland.

From Settle Market Place, walk around the back of the town hall into High Street, continuing past Lloyds Bank, the library and the Talbot Arms. Keep straight ahead into Chapel Square, heading towards Greenfoot Car Park. Take the tarmac path which winds to the left above and behind the car park, then between the bungalows to Ingfield Lane. Go right but almost immediately turn left onto an unsurfaced farm track — Brockhole Lane.

At a wooden gate, keep on the lower track (right) which winds its way past Fish Copy Barn and into Lodge Road at Hoyman Laithe Farm. Cross, now taking the first of a series of stone step- and gap-stiles ahead, crossing the next two fields, then alongside a wall, slowly climbing towards the wood ahead. At the next stile you enter Cleatop Wood.

An interpretive panel beyond the stile explains a little about this thirty acres (12 ha) of native woodland, owned and managed by the Woodland Trust, planted in 2003 over a site rich in archaeological and wildlife interest.

At a junction of paths, follow the lower, clearer path downhill to the next stile. Go left here, following the wall uphill to a gap on the left and wall corner. Ignore the gap but take the field-gate on the left (GR 818613). This leads onto a delightful permissive path into the

Mountain pansy.

5

heart of Cleatop Park. The path climbs through deciduous woodland, dominated by mature oak and beech trees, soon passing old earthworks. Eventually the path meets the narrower public path coming in on the right from Mearbeck (GR 821611).

Turn sharp left up a narrow path through the woods, with pine trees eventually dominating as you reach the crest of the hill. As the path descends it veers to the right to another stile (GR 821613) into open pasture. Head for Lodge Farm below, the path keeping to the wall corner below and alongside the wall to a gate onto the track above the farm. Turn right here, following the lane as it bears right. Keep right at the fork, heading uphill past Hudsa Plantation with Peart Crags to the left. As

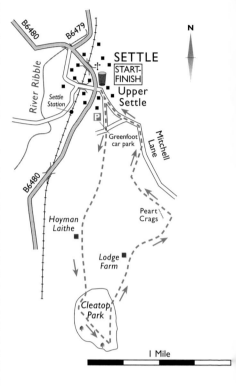

you near Black's Plantation (a small open area), a gate and signposted stile (GR 828623) reached by turning sharp left leads to a path which follows a stone wall to the right. A stone step-stile on the right crosses into a smaller field which descends to a slightly awkward pedestrian gate and stone stile (GR 824626). Turn sharp right. There are magnificent views across the rooftops of Settle.

Follow the path down, again alongside the wall which eventually bears right to merge into a grassy track, through gates, which leads into Mitchell Lane. Turn left. The market place is directly ahead.

The impressive Folly in Settle is a grand seventeenth-century merchant's house built in 1679 by Robert Preston. It now houses the excellent Museum of North Craven Life — well worth a visit if opening times coincide.

6

Giggleswick Scar

Distance: 6 miles (9.5 km)
Time: 3 hours
Terrain: tracks and field paths, some steep sections
Start: Settle Market Place, grid ref 820637   Maps: OS OL2, OL41
Parking: choice of public car parks in Settle
Refreshments/facilities: choice of inns and cafés in Settle;
toilets in car parks and at station
Public Transport: Settle-Carlisle line from Leeds and Skipton;
bus 580 from Skipton (not Sundays)

This walk through classic limestone country offers exceptionally fine views of both Penyghent and Ingleborough, but its most striking feature is the summit of Giggleswick Scar itself and the deep ravine of Buckhaw Brow seen from an unusual angle.

From Settle Market Place, walk past the town hall to the zebra crossing. Cross and go straight ahead along the narrow lane, Kirkgate, by the Singing Kettle Café and past some delightful eighteenth- and nineteenth-century terraced houses and courtyards. Immediately past Proctor House, look for a narrow alleyway, locally known as a 'ginnel' (the main clue is a No Cycling sign), which leads between house backs and alongside the railway line, going behind Whitefriars Car Park and under the railway viaduct. Turn left at the main road towards Giggleswick and past the schools and swimming pool, passing the entrance to Stackhouse Lane before reaching the Mains, a quiet suburban road. Follow the Mains as it ascends past pleasant housing. At the end of the road, where it narrows, continue through a gate into an enclosed track past woodland, soon offering fine views along upper Ribblesdale, the Settle-Carlisle Railway edging its way up the valley, and with the great rounded summit of Penyghent dominating the skyline.

The track soon begins to climb alongside woodland. At a fork, bear left up the main track (not the right of way but this is now public access land) which curves up alongside the woodland. Follow the main stony track, as it ascends and twists around an S-shaped curve now crossing open grassland, climbing up to the edge of the Giggleswick Quarry. Keep away from the locked gate and dangerous quarry face, but turn right, uphill, alongside the

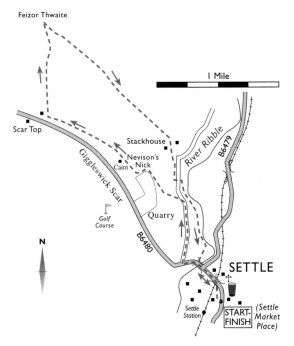

fence now joining the right of way from Giggleswick as it heads around and above this currently dormant limestone quarry.

If quarries are not usually scenic, here there are impressive views down into the great exposed Carboniferous Limestone strata that forms so much of the spectacular scenery of this part of Craven — and limestone remains an important local industrial product that maintains employment in the area.

At the top of the quarry, at a fork of paths (GR 809654) where a path on the left around the quarry fence climbs to a small cairn known as School Boy's Tower, take the path which forks slightly right, and which continues to climb the low ridge above Giggleswick Scar, soon heading through a natural gap in the limestone outcrops.

This is known as Nevison's Nick, a narrow pass over the Scar Top, linked to the legend of John Nevison, a well known seventeenth-century Yorkshire highwayman, known as Swift Nick, a Robin Hood-style figure allegedly robbing the rich to give to the poor. According to one local legend, a fairy spirit from nearby Giggleswick Well gave Nevison a magic bridle which enabled the highwayman and his horse to undertake prodigious feats of speed and daring — no doubt through this very rocky pass.

Take the path through the Nick, heading now along the top of the ridge. You can make a short diversion to another cairn on the edge of the scar, a fine viewpoint, looking across to the Forest of Bowland and Pendle Hill. Return to the main path, keeping ahead to a second cairn on the main path, with extensive views now into upper Ribblesdale, again with the round summit of Penyghent a main feature.

The path now descends slightly and comes to a high drystone wall without a crossing (GR 802657). Now take the narrow path left — not a right of way again but you are still on public access land — which follows the wall and begins to descend sharply down the side of the scar. A little care is needed here as the path zigzags across loose scree and stones to join the main path marked with a ladder-stile coming up on the left from Giggleswick. Almost hidden, in a deep ravine, is the former main A65 or old Kendal turnpike road climbing up Buckhaw Brow.

Cross the stile. Your path follows the top of the scar, ascending to another ladder-stile ahead and, as the gradient eases near the summit of Buckhaw Brow below, you reach a narrow ravine carrying a bridleway from the road. Turn right along the lip of the ravine, the path gradually dropping to meet the bridleway (GR 798659) which now bears left out of the hollow and through a bridle-gate, climbing past an old limekiln. Follow the bridleway, marked by gates, across a large enclosure, before following a wall side to the large enclosure of Feizor Thwaite. At a gate (GR 797669) a narrower informal path bears right to join the main grassy track between Feizor and Stackhouse. Follow this track to the right, ascending to a gate and stile. Keep in the same direction past another two gates, but taking care just beyond the third (GR 804665) to go through the gate on the right as the path now follows the other side of the wall.

Keep the same direction now, through more gates, until the faint track winds down over steep pasture when you will see, directly ahead and halfway down the hillside, a ladder-stile in the crossing wall below (GR 811657). This marks your line of path. Directly below is the hamlet of Stackhouse and a line of trees — a wooden fingerpost marks the path. Turn right here, the path now following the wall, and then the wall alongside Stackhouse Lane. At a stile (GR 814652) cross into the lane, taking the next stile almost directly opposite. This leads to an attractive path, part of the Ribble Way, across fields, through more stiles alongside the river, and then along an enclosed way past the school playing fields to emerge at Settle Bridge. Turn left for Settle town centre.

Victoria Cave

Distance: 4¹/₂ miles (7 km)
Time: 2¹/₂ hours
Terrain: tracks and field paths; two steep ascents make this a
short but relatively strenuous walk.
Start: Settle Market Place, grid ref 820637   Map: OS OL2
Parking: choice of car parks in Settle town centre
Refreshments/facilities: choice of inns and cafés in Settle; toilets
in car park and at station
Public transport: Settle-Carlisle line from Leeds or Skipton daily;
bus 580 from Skipton (not Sundays)

This walk to Victoria Cave, one of the most important archaeological sites in Craven, is notable for both dramatic limestone scenery and panoramic views across Ribblesdale.

From Settle Market Place, take the narrow road leading out of its north-east corner, Constitutional Hill, passing some fine Georgian houses and cottages as you do. The lane climbs before bearing right at a junction to become a steep, unsurfaced track, now carrying the Pennine Bridleway towards upper Ribblesdale and Malham. This is a steady climb, soon passing the entrance to Castlebergh Scar. At the gate where the enclosed track opens into pasture, take the grassy track used by most walkers which bears right up the slope — not the right of way but you are now on public access land.

A punishingly steep section now, so pause to enjoy the view back over the rooftops of Settle and Giggleswick and beyond to the flat-topped fells of the Forest of Bowland. At the drystone wall, cross through the wide gap before bearing right to join the signposted path coming up from below. Keep climbing uphill, parallel with the wall. Ignore a narrow path branching off to the left, but keep ahead up the steep brow of the hill.

Keep ahead towards the gateway ahead, passing increasing craggy outcrops on the left. You eventually cross over the brow of the hill into a broad, rocky amphitheatre between the hills, with the spectacular line of crags that form Warrendale Knotts rising high to your left.

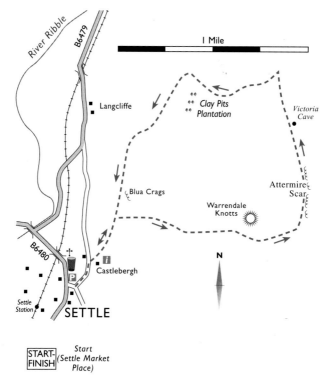

START-FINISH

Start
(Settle Market
Place)

Where the path forks, keep to the main path to the right (again not the right of way but the easier route through public access land) which goes through another gateway before descending, with the wall on your right, into a shallow hollow between the crags, the impressive limestone screes and crags looking like parts of much higher mountain slopes, a miniature Dolomite region in Ribblesdale.

Follow the path down into the floor of the shallow valley heading towards the step-stile below. Cross with care and keep ahead to where a steep side-valley formed by Attermire Scar comes in from your left (GR 839642). The path now forks to the left, leaving the main Malham route, and ascends a steep, rocky slope to the ladder-stile above. Cross, the path now following the far side of the wall to the left. Head up to the wall corner ahead and on the right to where a small kissing-gate gives access to the path below Brent Scar (GR 839648). Follow the path alongside the wall as it goes below past Victoria Cave, soon visible as a great dark chasm in the cliff face above.

11

A warning notice advising you not to go beyond the mouth of the cave stands at the bottom of the steep and narrow path (GR 837651) that goes back up the rocky slope to the mouth of the cave above. But it is a walk worth taking. Victoria Cave is a dramatic feature in its own right as well as a fine viewpoint across the dale.

Discovered by chance in 1837, the year of Queen Victoria's coronation, the cave has been thoroughly excavated over the decades since. Within the cave's thick clay deposits, an astonishing record of climate change in the Dales has been unearthed, extending over tens of thousands of years. Archaeological finds from an era when Ribblesdale enjoyed a tropical climate have been recovered, including bones of long-extinct animals, earliest finds going back 130,000 years and including hippos, narrow-nosed rhino, elephants and spotted hyenas.

After the last Ice Age some 12,000 years ago the cave was used as a shelter by brown bear, reindeer and other mammals. Evidence of the earliest human occupation comes from an 11,000-year-old antler harpoon point. There are also Roman and Romano-British artefacts, suggesting the cave has been used for storage and possibly even for a shrine over millennia.

In recent years the roof of the cave has become increasingly unstable and, because of the danger of roof falls, visitors without the necessary safety equipment and supervision are strongly advised by the national park authority (who manage the site) not to go inside.

Return to the main footpath, following it to another kissing-gate. This leads back onto the Pennine Bridleway Settle Loop heading along the Gorbeck road towards Malham (GR 837653). Turn left here, descending past Clay Pits Plantation to where the path joins the tarmac road to Malham Tarn. Almost immediately, on the left, a field-gate gives access to the continuation of the Pennine Bridleway. This goes below Clay Pits Plantation, and then becomes a lovely terraced path.

Enjoy the magnificent views across upper Ribblesdale, towards Smearsett Scar and beyond to Ingleborough summit, the village of Langcliffe with its former mill immediately below.

Follow the bridleway, through kissing-gates and past a small wood, descending below Blua Crags to meet the path from Settle. Keep ahead through the next gate to rejoin the path to Attermire, and the enclosed track down to Settle's Constitution Hill and the market place.

Stainforth Force

Distance: 4¹/₂ miles (7 km)
Time: 2¹/₂ hours
Terrain: Tracks, field and riverside paths; one long steep section;
some fairly steep stiles
Start and parking: Stainforth car park, grid ref 821672
Map: OS OL2
Refreshments/facilities: Craven Heifer Inn, Stainforth; shop in
Langcliffe; Sunday afternoon teas usually in Langcliffe Village
Institute on summer weekends; toilets in Stainforth car park
Public Transport: Bus B1 from Settle (not Sundays); this walk can
also be joined from Settle at Langcliffe by taking the traffic-free
lane from the top of Constitution Hill to Langcliffe village

This walk links two very fine, contrasting Craven waterfalls: the foaming white waters of Stainforth Force at the end of the walk; and the pencil-slim, almost hidden Catrigg Force near the start; whilst the walk around the old mill pond at Langcliffe Mill is also memorable.

From Stainforth car park, walk into the village. Turn right along the main street past the Craven Heifer Inn. Cross the bridge over Stainforth Beck, at the far side of which a path follows the beck towards the village green. Follow the lane past the green and cottages as it bears sharply right, up Goat Scar Lane.

This old fell track and packhorse way has been recently resurfaced and restored as part of the Pennine Bridleway.

The first section of the lane is a steep but steady climb for about half a mile (800 m) before the gradient gradually eases over the brow of the hill. Before reaching a field-gate at the end of the lane, look for the footpath through a pedestrian gate on the left (GR 832670), signed Catrigg Force, which leads down a narrow, stony path towards pine trees below. Take the little pedestrian gate on the left, leading to steps down to a relatively level area.

From here you have a splendid view of Catrigg Upper Force – the slender, column of water of Catrigg Beck. There is the smaller Lower Force below which requires some careful negotiation of a narrower path to see properly — a little care needed here.

Return the way you came up to Goat Scar Lane, this time going through the field-gate and following the broad, recently resurfaced track, the Pennine Bridleway, which heads right, due south, towards a second gate ahead. Keep right again here. Follow the Pennine Bridleway signs to join a clearer track which curves right between walls heading for the gate at Upper Winskill Farm (GR 829665). Do not go through here, but now leave the Pennine Bridleway to take the track directly ahead, still between walls and waymarked, towards Little Winskill.

As the track curves to the right and the white farmhouse of Little Winskill comes into view, look for a narrow step-stile and pedestrian gate on your left (GR 828664). Cross. The path now heads across the field to another stile and gate in the field corner. Turn right here alongside the wall, the path now heading down through scattered woodland to a pedestrian gate. Your path now winds down a steep slope at the end of Langliffe Scar, soon curving to the left down Dick Ground Plantation.

There are spectacular views down Ribblesdale towards Langliffe village from here. Superb medieval ploughing strips or lynchets are clearly visible in the fields ahead, as well as the enclosed track towards Langcliffe you will eventually join.

The path now swings right, crossing a stile into a long field before joining the enclosed track to Langcliffe at a gate. A pleasant walk now, between fields, ascending slightly before dropping into pretty Langcliffe village with its scatter of cottages and chapel around the village green. Keep in the same direction through the village before bearing right to the main B6160 road.

Cross carefully, taking the narrow path slightly to your right (GR 821650), a stone slab marking the entrance to the enclosed path between walls down to a footbridge over the Settle-Carlisle railway. Cross.

At the junction outside Langcliffe Place Caravan site, keep straight on towards the eighteenth-century former cotton and paper mill directly ahead. Keep to the path on the right, behind the yellow fence and markings. The mill is due to be converted

Golden plover.

14

into a hotel in the near future, but the right of way will be maintained. It leads alongside the main mill building, emerging below the mill dam before turning right up steps alongside the mill pond. A spectacular stretch follows as the path bridges the old mill race and goes alongside the mill pond before twisting left to pass a group of cottages known locally as the Locks. Turn left just past the cottages across the metal footbridge above Langcliffe's spectacular weir, noting the special salmon leap on the right-hand-side of the falls.

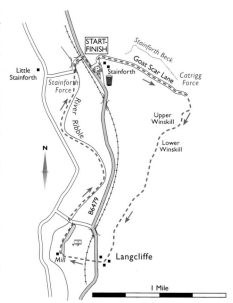

At the far side of the bridge, join the Ribble Way over the step-stile on the right. This is a pretty section of riverside path, easy to follow, keeping close to the river below woodland, past Langcliffe High Mill. Where the river enters a narrow gorge, the path bears left up steps to twin stiles. Cross, bearing slightly right with the river to cross a streamlet emerging from a spring. As the Stainforth caravan site comes into view, the path crosses the stile right and follows the riverside to emerge at Stainforth Force.

This lovely shimmering waterfall is a favourite place for picnickers and strollers any time of the year. Directly ahead is the slender-arched Stainforth Packhorse Bridge, built in the late seventeenth century, which connects Little or Knight Stainforth with the rest of the village, but which also used to carried packhorse trains across the Pennines between Lancaster and York. The bridge is now owned and maintained by the National Trust.

Cross the stile at the bridge, turning right to follow the lane to the main road and turn right. Stainforth village lies just ahead, but to avoid crossing the busy main road, look for the gate just beyond the Old School (now a private house) which gives access to a small picnic area and a tunnel under the road by the beck, which leads directly to the car park and centre of the village.

Helwith Bridge

Distance: 6 miles (9.5 km)
Time: 3 hours
Terrain: Riverside and field paths and moorland; easy apart from one long (half mile/800 m) steep ascent.
Start: Horton village, grid ref 808726   Map: OS OL2
Parking: large public car park in Horton-in-Ribblesdale
Refreshments/facilities: two pubs and two cafés in Horton-in-Ribblesdale; pub at Helwith Bridge; toilets in Horton
Public transport: Settle-Carlisle line from Leeds or Skipton daily; bus B1 from Settle (not Sundays)

A lovely section of the Ribble Way precedes the climb along Long Lane which offers spectacular views of Penyghent, Ingleborough and the great rock facades of upper Ribblesdale which even a century and a half of intensive quarry activity have not tamed.

From Horton car park, cross in front of the toilet block and grassy verge to the wooden footbridge over the river. Just past the end of the bridge a step-stile on the left leads down to the riverside path, signed 'Cragghill Farm'. (If coming from Horton Station — with its impressive views of Penyghent as you descend from the station — walk down the station drive, cross to the lane towards the village, to reach the stile in the wall, right, before the car park bridge.)

Follow this pleasant riverside path, with views of the Settle-Carlisle line to your right, soon crossing a stile and along the top of a concrete pipe. Bear right at the next stile and footbridge over a ditch, continuing downstream past a small sewage works to another stile. Go through a line of trees, keeping ahead (ignoring the footbridge over the river which is a short cut back to Horton) towards Cragghill Farm.

Through the metal field-gate, cross the track to the next field-gate and continue along the track between wire fences ahead, which follows the river before entering a large open pasture. Your way is half-right here, following the signpost, directly ahead across a large field to where a ladder-stile leads

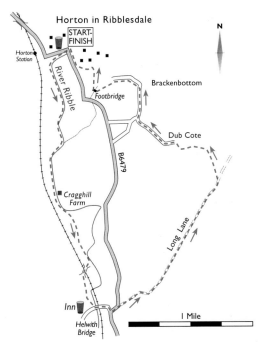

Horton in Ribblesdale

START-FINISH

Horton Station

River Ribble

Footbridge

Brackenbottom

Dub Cote

B6479

Cragghill Farm

Long Lane

Inn

Helwith Bridge

N

1 Mile

to a path parallel to an old flooded enclosed track (GR 809704). Keep ahead along the path over another stile to where on the left the path goes over a stile to rejoin the lane, now by no means dry but a little less flooded, though there are usually a couple of deep pools to bypass. The track passes another footbridge. Ignore, but follow the track as it swings right and goes under the railway to enter the access road to Foredale quarry.

Directly ahead is a wooden kissing-gate that takes walkers along a parallel path away from quarry lorries which often thunder through on weekdays. Follow the path for some 200 yards to where it comes to a crossing of paths at a wooden fence. Go left over the stile and cross the lane to the stile in the fence opposite. Bear left here across a small enclosure towards the Helwith Bridge Inn, a walker-friendly pub straight ahead. A stile at the side of the pub leads into the lane.

Turn left here, walking on the right-hand verge to avoid traffic, and head across Helwith Bridge towards the road junction. Cross the main B6479, carefully avoiding fast-moving traffic, to enter the enclosed track which leaves the main road that now swings left towards Horton.

This is Long Lane, a typical Pennine fell track that climbs in a straight line, due north-westwards. The track bends round past the junction with Moor Head Lane that takes the Ribble Way south-westwards towards Stainforth. Keep up the main track, a long, slow slog compensated at every step — in good weather — by spectacular views.

Geologists will note here the contrast between the classic Great Scar Limestone directly opposite, gouged out in huge terraces by the huge quarrying operations at Horton Quarry, with the darker, much more ancient outcrops and quarry faces further south where far more ancient Silurian slates are extracted for use as tough stone for surfacing roads all over the north of England.

Even more impressive are the views across to the ever-emerging panorama of Ingleborough, and Simon and Park fells, as you ascend, with the tips of Whernside and Blea Moor coming into view, and the great sweep of the Bowland Fells beyond the dale to the south.

The gradient eases very slightly as you cross through a field-gate, the village of Horton-in-Ribblesdale and its church in the distance below you. Continue past a shallow ford to the next gate, 150 yards beyond which (GR 826710) a wooden footpath sign indicates the start of a lovely green way which leaves Long Lane to descend gently, along the hillside, towards Dub Cote Farm below. The track broadens and descends towards a wall. Do not go through the gate ahead, but take the ladder-stile over the wall below left (GR 825714). This gives access to a faint grassy path, which follows the wall before bearing to the left and curving down the hillside to join a broader vehicle track that descends towards the farm. Cross the stile at the farm to enter the track that passes the farm and meets a tarmac lane.

Follow this quiet, narrow lane, dominated by views of Penyghent summit to your right, as it winds between pastures. At a T-junction, turn right. Head past Brackenbottom Farm, where you might be surprised to discover a falconry centre. You now join the inevitably busy Three Peaks Walk for a few hundred yards. Continue until the primary school. Just beyond, a footbridge, right, crosses the stream from Douk Ghyll Cave. Cross, turning right for a few yards to where an enclosed track bears left past a farm. This reaches Horton Scar Lane, another enclosed track, this time carrying the Pennine Way.

Turn left here into the village — the welcoming Crown Inn is on your right, and Penyghent Café and the Golden Lion Inn on your left. Turn right for the car park and toilets, and back over the footbridge and up the hill to the railway station.

Crummackdale

> **Distance: 5 miles (8 km)**
> **Time: 3 hours**
> **Terrain: mainly field paths but with a large number of steep**
> **ladder-stiles; two moderate ascents**
> **Start: Austwick village, grid ref 767684 Maps: OS OL2, OL41**
> **Parking: Austwick village centre; please park responsibly**
> **Refreshment: Game Cock Inn and Traddock Guest House in**
> **Austwick (lunches), Feizor Refreshment (lunches and light**
> **snacks); no public toilets in Austwick.**
> **Public Transport: bus 581 from Settle and Ingleton (not Sundays)**

This is a richly rewarding walk into Crummackdale, within its five miles offering some spectacular limestone features and memorable views of two of the Three Peaks from less familiar angles.

From the crossroads in the centre of Austwick, take the Settle road south-eastwards for about 300 yards. Cross the bridge over Austwick Beck to a bend in the road where a narrow farm track, Wood Lane, leads off to the left. Follow this for a quarter of a mile to where a ladder-stile on the right leads into a field. Keep straight ahead, skirting grassy mounds, to another ladder-stile in the wall ahead leading into Hale Lane, a narrow enclosed packhorse way. The path continues over the next stile ahead, and now crosses a series of fields, the path marked by ladder-stiles ahead. You soon pass the entrance into Oxenber Wood Nature Reserve on the left. Keep ahead over the stiles towards Feizor.

Three fields before Feizor (GR 787678) the paths split. The ladder-stile in the wall above left takes the path directly towards Wharfe Wood, crossing up to a pedestrian gate and stile in the far right-hand corner of the next field leading to a tarmac track. Turn left here.

But if you want to call into the pretty hamlet of Feizor, a settlement on the old Lancaster-York packhorse way, to visit Feizor Refreshments for lunch or home-made scones, cross the series of stiles directly ahead, turning left at the lane to Home Barn. The lane passes the farm and swings left through the

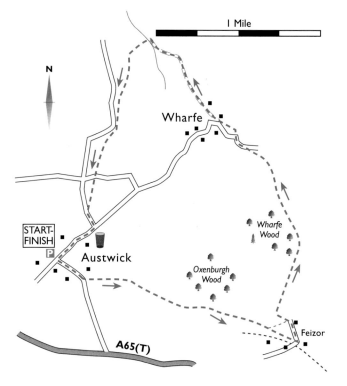

hamlet, through a field-gate to rejoin the path previously described from Austwick.

Follow this track as it climbs through a narrow natural pass or shallow ravine, past limestone crags and even small caves, to the summit of the pass.

On a clear day there are breathtakingly beautiful views of the sphinx-like shape of Penyghent to the right, with the long, flat summit of Fountains Fell beyond and the spectacular limestone crags of Moughton Scar and Moughton Nab directly ahead.

Some 250 yards down the hillside (GR 791685), a stile on the left, signed to Wharfe, leads to a lovely path down to Wharfe Gill. Go through gateways by the corner of Wharfe Wood below, and follow the wall alongside the wood down the hillside, then over more ladder-stiles. Cross a track and over a stone step-stile to pass by a little ford (GR 788691). Keep ahead over two small wooden footbridges before descending to the lane from Helwith Bridge at another stile.

Turn left along the lane towards Wharfe hamlet, but at the first junction take the track right towards a cottage. Go left at the cottage, then first right up a delightful, narrow, grassy enclosed way between stone walls that climbs behind the hamlet. This joins the main track enclosed between stone walls now turning northwards into Crummackdale.

The ring ouzel is also known as the 'mountain blackbird'.

As the track ascends gently, the views ahead are now dominated by the great ridge and flat summit of Ingleborough. Keep ahead to the crest of the hill, before this ancient packhorse way descends into the shallow valley formed by Austwick Beck. At a junction of paths, take the broader path left which drops down to pass a grassy area by the beck, with a couple of rather fine stone clapper bridges and shallow waterfalls.

This is Wash Dub where Austwick Beck forms a natural pool used for many years for sheep washing. This is now an informal access area, with repair work on the ancient bridges completed thanks to the support of the Yorkshire Dales Millennium Trust. The bench here makes a perfect picnic place.

You can cross either bridge and walk up the lane, or up the grassy hillside for some fifty yards to a little wooden pedestrian gate (GR 776705) reached through a gap (left) from the lane. The path, faint on the ground, now climbs steadily past unusual slab-like stone outcrops, before turning due south. Aim for the summit of the low hill ahead. Keep your direction, looking for a low mound in the summit where a pole indicates the whereabouts of a stone step-stile (GR 774703). The path now descends in the same direction, marked by ladder-stiles, crossing a track to Sowerthwaite Farm, then down to the corner of Crummack Lane.

Head for the stile just to the west of the barn below, where a little wooden footbridge crosses a beck (Norber Sike) to the next stile. Keep alongside the wall to cross twin stiles over Thwaite Lane. Follow the wall down to another stile and through a complex of buildings at Town Head Farm.

This leads into the lower end of Crummack Lane. Keep left to emerge at the eastern end of Austwick. Turn right to the village centre and bus stop and shelter, or your parked car.

The Norber Erratics

Distance: 4¹/₂ miles (7 km)
Time: 2¹/₂ hours
Terrain: tracks and field paths; one steep section
Start: Clapham village, grid ref 745692   Map: OL2
Parking: Clapham village car park
Refreshment: inn, cafés, toilets in Clapham; inn in Austwick
Public Transport: bus 581 from Skipton (summer Sundays)

A walk that includes one of the most dramatic natural geological features in the whole of the Yorkshire Dales.

Walk up this most attractive of Dales villages, keeping to the right of Clapham Beck, along Gildersbank, past the entrance to Ingleborough Hall (now an outdoor education centre) towards the handsome, mainly Regency, church. Bear right to follow the stony track between churchyard and estate wall to the right of the church. Go right again to enter the first of twin tunnels, designed to screen the ancient, pre-turnpike road, Thwaite Lane, from the landscaped park of the hall. Once through the tunnels the gradient soon eases, and you pass woodland and the Long Lane junction, with increasingly fine views across to the Bowland Fells on your right. After about half a mile (1 km) you reach and cross a ladder-stile on the left (GR 760692). This bears half-right towards the massive bulk of Robin Proctor's Scar ahead.

Take care to fork right before the scar, making for the wall corner on the right and a ladder-stile. Head along the narrow path which leads up the slope ahead past the footpath signpost through jagged limestone crags. Ascend to the summit of a plateau (GR 766698), to enter a strange boulder field.

These dark boulders are the famous Norber Erratics, ancient Silurian rocks carried here by the Crummackdale glacier from the top of the valley and deposited here as the ice melted some 13,000 years ago. There are scores of these great boulders of varying sizes, some perched precariously on curious pedestals of much younger Carboniferous Limestone.

Enjoying the fine views, return to the lower path. But now bear left towards the stile in the wall above Nappa Scars (GR 766697) to follow the path

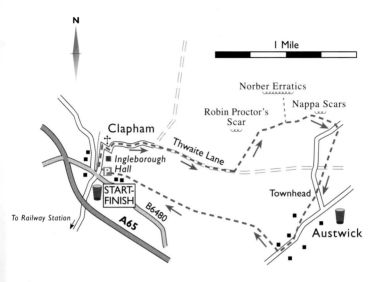

which descends and turns left to go below the scars. Continue along the top of the narrow green ledge to a ladder-stile into the lane at Norber Brow (GR 773696). Cross the lane to the next ladder-stile ahead. Turn right to walk downhill across open pasture.

Head for a tiny footbridge over Norber Sike Beck, to the right of a small farm building. Beyond is another stile. Cross here and follow the wall up to another narrow lane to Slaindale, where twin stiles lead to the path alongside the wall to cottages at Town Head Farm. Go over the stile here and into Crummack Lane. Continue left downhill to Austwick village centre.

Turn right and walk through the village, past pub, road junction and bus stop, to where, on the right between houses, a stone step-stile (GR 766684) indicates the start of the path back to Clapham.

This curves gently up the field to another stile past a bench, up to and behind a wooded knoll and then through a succession of fields, continuing along the edge of a large pasture up to a metal kissing-gate into the parkland of the Ingleborough Estate. Follow the metal estate fence through a gate to eventually reach the farm. Follow the enclosed footpath (waymarked) to the right of the main farm drive, keeping with the waymarks again slightly right to join another narrow enclosed path. This emerges behind the car park at the public toilets in the centre of Clapham village.

Clapdale & Trow Gill

Distance: 5 miles (8 km)
Time: 2¹/₂ hours
Terrain: mainly stony tracks; one steady steep climb
Start: Clapham village, grid ref 745692   Map: OS OL2
Parking: Clapham village car park
Refreshments/facilities: inn, cafés and public toilets in Clapham
Public transport: bus 581 from Settle (weekdays), Ingleborough
Pony bus (summer Sundays); trains from Leeds and Skipton to
Clapham Station (1¹/₂ miles/2 km from start)

A walk through the narrow picturesque valley of Clapdale and a spectacular limestone gorge onto the shoulder of Ingleborough, returning via lonely Clapham Bottoms and Long Lane.

From Clapham's old market cross or car park, walk up the right-hand side of Clapham Beck to the stone footbridge over the beck. Cross. Turn right to the top of the village, looking right to the pretty, if man-made, waterfall emerging from the lake dam. Go under the fine new entrance arch emblazoned 'Cave & Trail' into the Ingleborough Estate, paying the admission fee (currently 60p) at the machine at the entrance. This doesn't give change so have the right coins with you. You can avoid paying the charge by taking the public bridleway which leads to the left up and behind the estate woods to Clapdale Farm before rejoining the valley near Ingleborough Cave, but this misses one of the highlights of the walk, Clapdale Lake.

The lake was created as a scenic feature and source of early hydroelectric power by the Farrer family in the nineteenth century. Some of the woodland planting across the lake was originally laid out by the great botanist and plant collector Reginald Farrer between 1916 and 1920, but this has been added to in recent years by using species of native trees. The Drive was built in Victorian times to bring visitors by horse-drawn vehicle from Clapham Railway Station to Ingleborough Cave.

You soon pass an ornate limestone shelter know as the Grotto. At the gate beyond the woods the little valley opens out. Head for Ingleborough Cave some 400 yards ahead.

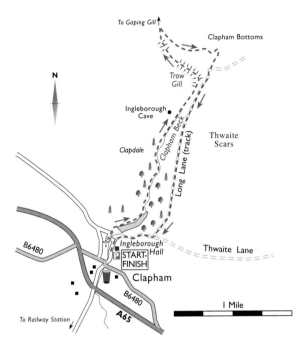

On most days of the year there are tours every hour of this remarkable floodlit cave, giving a superb insight into the spectacular and extensive cave systems that lie underneath so much of the Yorkshire Dales.

Continue along the track above the cave, through the gate ahead and ascend into the ever-narrowing gorge of Trow Gill. Beyond the next gate this soon becomes a steep and rocky way. The great rockfaces of Carboniferous Limestone, crowned by pine and larch trees, come ever closer to the path, and the way soon narrows to be little more than an arms' span in width, more a rocky scramble than a path.

Climb to the top of this dramatic gorge. The path continues to climb, following a stone wall, left, through a shallower gorge. Follow this upwards for about half a mile (1km) to the second stile, a double wooden structure on the left (GR 752724). Unless you are tempted to follow the main path to Gaping Gill and the summit of Ingleborough, you should now turn sharp right to locate a grassy path leading across a low hilly plateau behind, soon with extensive views over the Bowland Fells. This is shown as a faint dotted line on the OS Explorer map and starts as a broad path heading due

Flowers of the limestone uplands: bloody cranesbill, rusty-back fern, twayblade, Helicella itala and hart's-tongue fern.

south-eastwards, winding between grass-covered sinkholes or shallow potholes. This is not a right of way but a path across public access land.

As you reach an outcrop of limestone on the right, follow the path sharp right for about eighty yards (the trees directly ahead are actually the woods at the top of Trow Gill). Now follow the narrow path which turns sharp left, alongside a narrow, sunken limestone wall, with little more than jagged foundation stones remaining. Where this path peters out as a sheep path, keep straight ahead. Soon bear left (GR 757718) to begin to descend the hillside at an angle to ease the gradient down to the broad, grassy-covered dry valley floor of Clapham Bottoms below you.

If you look ahead you will see, on the opposite hillside, a vehicle track angling up to a gate above right. Descend to the valley floor (GR 758720) towards a pothole enclosed by a barbed-wire fence ahead. Ignore the path back along the valley floor, which would take you back into Trow Gill, Instead, go to a crossing of paths below the enclosed pothole to pick up the vehicle track climbing up to your right. Follow the track up the shoulder of the hill. You reach two gates in the wall ahead. Take the gate on the left (GR 758716) which leads into Long Lane, a public bridleway.

Long Lane's name is self-evident as you follow this fine enclosed track. It dips below Thwaite Scar, with impressive views below you to your right down into Clapdale and the route you followed into Trow Gill.

Straight, easy walking now, following the lane for over a mile (2 km) as it descends by Thwaite Plantation and climbs back up to the junction with Thwaite Lane, now part of the Pennine Bridleway. Turn right here, soon descending through twin tunnels under Ingleborough Hall Park to emerge in Clapham village behind the church. Turn left for the car park and bus stop.

26

Storrs Common

Distance: 3¹/₂ miles (6 km)
Time: 2 hours
**Terrain: tracks, field paths and a section of quiet lane; one steep
ascent over rough common land; and some stepping stones which
are fun in normal conditions but which can be tricky after wet
weather if the River Doe is in spate — check the level of the river
at Ingleton Bridge before starting out**
Start: Ingleton Community Centre, grid ref 695730   Map: OL2
Parking: Ingleton car park, by community centre and bus stop
**Refreshments/facilities: choice of facilities in Ingleton; toilets in
car park and in riverside park en route**
**Public Transport: buses 581 from Settle (Monday to Saturday
only) and Ingleborough Pony (summer Sundays)**

*Even if it can't quite match the incomparable beauty of Ingleton's famous
Waterfall Walk, this alternative route to Beezleys offers several features of
interest around the village of Ingleton itself and with magnificent views of
Ingleborough.*

From the bus stop and main car park outside Ingleton Community Centre,
head towards the disused railway viaduct. Bear right past the toilet block
and recycling bins, behind which a path twists down steps to the road
towards the village centre. Cross, but then take the gap-stile almost directly
opposite. Turn right, down steps, into a cul-de-sac lane past a row of
terraced houses. Keep right past the houses. Fork right again past a white
cottage and little garden to what seems to be a high stone wall. As you get
closer you will see stone steps half-hidden in the wall corner. These bring
you out at the end of Ingleton Bridge. Cross the road.

Slightly to the right, a path (marked 'Heated Pool') leads behind the bridge
wall to a riverside walk. Pass the site of Ingleton's old mill, and the village
swimming pool, before curving uphill to the right past a picnic area and
small park, emerging in Sammy Lane by the youth hostel. Turn left at the
crossroads past the chip shop and along Thaking Lane, another narrow cul-
de-sac, this time with impressive views across the narrow gorge of the River

Doe. This narrows to a footpath, through a gate. At a fork, take the wider but less well-used track to the right (the path on the left is the exit of the Waterfalls Walk). This climbs steadily uphill, past an old, grassed-over quarry, before eventually emerging on the Hawes road at a white house, Rock Cottage.

Cross the road to pick up the line of a faint green track heading towards an outcrop of rock ahead (GR 703734). As you get close you will see a faint path winding its way on a strip of grass between the rocks. This is not a right of way, but there is full public access over this part of Storrs Common. Make your way steadily uphill, keeping the same direction over rough grazing. Over the brow of the hill, as the gradient eases, note the wall sloping in on your left. Now head for the far corner of the wall ahead and to the left where it joins the main footpath from Ingleton to Ingleborough (GR 705733).

Follow this usually busy stony track — a main route to Ingleborough summit — steadily uphill as it ascends between walls, curving to the right over the foothills of Ingleborough. At a stile and small pedestrian gate on the left, signed to Skirwith (GR 710734), cross and follow the field wall down to a ladder-stile on your left. Cross, and continue down the wall side to another stile onto the main Hawes road.

Directly opposite is a field-gate with a smaller pedestrian gate to its right. Don't be put off by the warning signs 'Danger Deep Excavation' but keep on the clearly marked path signed to Beezleys. This crosses a tiny stream, then turns sharp right to follow a gravel path alongside of trees planted to screen the quarry edge – the care taken by Ingleton Quarry to look after walkers is commendable.

At the pedestrian gate at the quarry entrance, cross the main entrance road with care over a pedestrian crossing, to the gate marked 'Public footpath' straight opposite. Turn left down the path between fences. Keep ahead where the path opens into a broader track heading for the gate and stile ahead.

You now enter a broad, sloping field. Keep half-right along a faint green track, descending between the wooden power cable pylons crossing a shallow stream. Where a field-gate comes into view in the wall, below left, head for this, to join a track that twists down to the River Doe at a ford (GR 707748). Just before the ford, a narrow path branches off left to a stile which leads to the stepping stones. These are level and well-constructed, and easy to cross at most times of the year, but should be avoided when the river is in flood and the stones are covered with water.

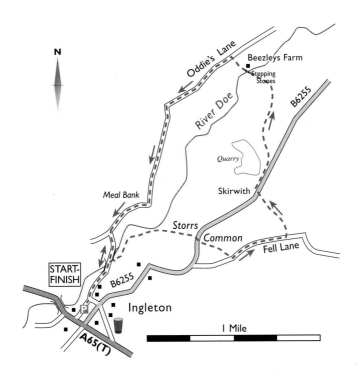

Follow the track up to Beezleys Farm, enjoying fine views back across to Ingleborough summit from here. Beezleys is on the return leg of the busy Waterfall Walk but this is only accessible for ticket holders.

There are in fact two public rights of way from Beezleys towards Ingleton shown on the map but neither is waymarked, they lack clear stiles and are currently difficult to negotiate, and may even be partly blocked by new tree planting. The easier and more practical option is therefore to proceed up to Oddie's Lane, which has little more than local traffic, and turn left for a walk of just over a mile back down into Ingleton.

There are fine views across the rooftops of Ingleton village as you descend and as the lane curves through attractive woodland above Meal Bank Quarry. Turn left at the T-junction to cross the bridge and continue up the hill to the village centre for shops, pubs and cafés, with the main car park and bus stop two minutes' walk to your right.

Ribblehead Viaduct

Distance: 5 miles (8 km)
Time: 2½ hours
**Terrain: tracks and quiet lanes, with a section of rough moorland
of over a mile, and a half mile along a busy roadside verge**
Start: Ribblehead Station, grid ref 765790   Map: OL2
**Parking: limited roadside parking at the B6255/6477 crossroads at
Ribblehead — public transport option is strongly recommended;
parking at the station is for rail customers only**
**Refreshments/facilities: Station Inn, Ribblehead (toilets available
for customers only)**
**Public Transport: Settle-Carlisle line from Leeds, Skipton or Settle
to Ribblehead; Ingleton Pony bus on summer Sundays**

*Ribblehead Viaduct, the most famous railway viaduct in England, dominates
the first part of this walk, its massive scale dwarfed by the huge outline of
Whernside. The return section crosses the edge of Ingleborough National
Nature Reserve.*

*By far the pleasantest way of reaching Ribblehead is by train as the journey
forms an integral part of the day's experience. The beautifully restored*

Ribblehead Viaduct.

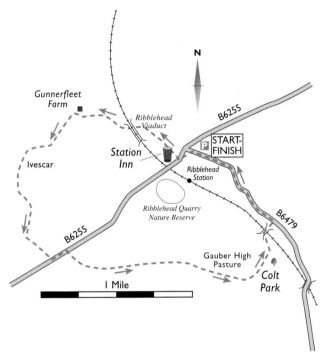

station now contains a small but fascinating visitor centre dedicated to the history of the Settle-Carlisle Railway.

From the station drive, head down to the B6255. Turn right past the Station Inn over the cattle grid to where a public bridleway signposted 'Bridleway', left, leads along a stony track towards the great viaduct itself.

Built between 1870 and 1874, and a quarter of a mile (402 metres) long, its twenty-four great stone arches rise up to 104 feet (32 m) above the wild moorland traversed by the railway line. It is a magnificent feat of Victorian railway engineering, a high point of the Settle-Carlisle line and a major landscape feature in its own right, within the spectacular setting of the Three Peaks. In particular the immense whaleback shape of Whernside here forms a magnificent natural backcloth, landscape and engineering both on a heroic scale. As various small interpretive panels will confirm, you pass the site of the Batty Moss Shanty Towns where, during the building of the viaduct and nearby Blea Moor Tunnel, over 2,000 navvies and their families lived, in conditions which had much in common with America's Wild West.

Follow the stony track under the awesome central arches of the viaduct, with the great flat-topped, stepped summit of Ingleborough asserting its presence seen through the arches ahead.

Keep ahead towards the outbuildings of Gunnerfleet Farm. Go through a gate before reaching and crossing Winterscales Beck. At a T-junction, turn left along the farm track through another gate and along a shallow valley. This soon joins the farm road from Ivescar. Keep left again, over another bridge, before ascending a low hillock and winding down to Low Sleights Road, the main B6255.

Turn left once more, and walk along the road (on the right-hand side to face often fast moving traffic). After 200 yards, a stile on the right signed 'Colt Park' leads into a farm track. Follow this track alongside the wall past a barn. After 150 yards, opposite a small limestone pavement outcrop (GR 754781), a faint track bears off left. This heads almost due east before ascending the gentle curve of the hillside over rough grazing and limestone outcrops. You will see a ladder-stile in the wall ahead. Keep the same direction, now winding your way through limestone pavement known as Sleights Pasture Rocks, a small plantation to your left, making your way carefully between the deep clints of Fell Close Rocks. As you come around the hillside the characteristic shape of the third and smallest peak, Penyghent, comes increasingly to dominate the view to the south-east. Continue over further stiles ahead (GR 763781), now contouring round towards a cottage and plantation, through a pedestrian gate into New Close. Descend slightly to join a track at Colt Park, on the edge of an especially beautiful corner of the Ingleborough National Nature Reserve.

Turn left on the farm track which winds between walls, crosses the bridge over the railway line and emerges at the main B6479 Gauber Road. Turn left. There is now an unavoidable half mile along this busy road. Walk on the right, single file, to face the traffic. For most of the way there is a grassy verge as sanctuary which broadens in places, passing Gauber Farm and a layby. As the viaduct comes back into view, some hundred yards before the junction, bear left along the wallside across an area of open common back to the welcoming Station Inn.

The Station Inn is a popular walkers' pub with good food and local real ale available most times of the day, whilst awaiting your train — and also the only local toilets (for customers only). It's also the only pub I know which has times of departing trains posted above the bar. If you have an hour to spare before your train, you might also have a stroll around the waymarked trail through the fascinating Ribblehead Quarry Nature Reserve, reached along the old quarry access road immediately beyond the railway line.

REG

CW00409083

PETER ROBSON

Newby Books

Current style (pages 5-13)   *Old-style (pages 14-24)*

Diplomatic (pages 33-37)   *Q series (page 27)*

European (pages 54-63)   *Age-related (pages 48-49)*

Welcome to
CAR REGISTRATION GUIDE (2nd Edition)

Vehicle registration in the UK began officially on 1 January 1904, though the earliest known actual issue was by Hastings Borough Council on 23 November 1903 (DY 1). From then until August 2001 the original 'old-style' registrations were issued first by county and county borough councils and subsequently by local offices of the DVLA. The 'current-style' system (two letters, two digits, three letters) was introduced in September 2001.

Since this 'Guide' was originally published in 2008 there have been several important changes which have necessitated a new edition. Perhaps the most significant of these was the closure of regional local licensing offices in Great Britain (2013) and Northern Ireland (2014). Registration marks are now organised for the whole of the UK from the Licensing Centre in Swansea (see page 76) but the area codes (first two letters of the mark) still relate to places of issue. As the exact locations of the former offices are now irrelevant I have reverted in the check list (pages 8 to 13) to the original names for Hull, Middlesbrough, Reading and districts of London as these are better-known than Beverley, Stockton, Theale, Borehamwood, Sidcup and Wimbledon.

Another government innovation has been the introduction of numerical trade plates which do not include an area code. These will gradually replace the older-format plates.

In the Irish Republic the registration system has also been modified. From 2013 the years have been divided into two six-month periods (January to June, July to December) with 1 or 2 added to the year identifier, e.g. 152 – for the second half of 2015. Trade plates, however, are not affected by this rule.

This new edition contains an expanded European section with descriptions and illustrations of private passenger car number plates for every country. There is also a page devoted to Gulf Arab states registrations in view of the rising number of supercars from that area visiting the UK.

Best wishes.

Peter Robson

Peter Robson
June 2015

3

WHERE REGISTRATION MARKS ARE ISSUED

Locations of former licensing offices* in U.K. (closed 2013/4) and offices in Channel Islands and Isle of Man

Inverness•
Aberdeen•
•Dundee
Glasgow •Edinburgh
Londonderry •Coleraine
•Ballymena
Omagh •Newcastle
Enniskillen •Belfast Carlisle
Armagh •Middlesbrough
Downpatrick
Isle of Man
•Preston Leeds •Hull
Manchester •Sheffield
Bangor Chester Lincoln
•Nottingham
Shrewsbury Birmingham •Norwich
•Peterborough
•Northampton •Ipswich
Worcester• •Luton
Swansea Oxford• •Chelmsford
Cardiff Reading•
Bristol •Maidstone
Portsmouth• •Brighton
Exeter• Bournemouth S.W. London S.E. London
•Truro N.W. London
• Alderney
Guernsey O•
Jersey

*Hull,
London North-West,
London South-East,
London South-West,
Middlesbrough and
Reading had been
either relocated or
renamed (Beverley,
Borehamwood, Sidcup,
Wimbledon, Stockton
and Theale respectively)
by the time of
closure in 2013.

In September 2001 the current style of registration mark was introduced in Great Britain (England, Wales and Scotland). Marks consist of **two letters, two digits** (numbers), **three letters**.

The first letter (Local Memory Tag) shows which region of Great Britain the mark comes from.

A	Anglia	**L**	London
B	Birmingham	**M**	Manchester and
C	Cymru (Wales)		Merseyside
D	Deeside and	**N**	North-east England
	Shrewsbury	**O**	Oxford
E	Essex	**P**	Preston and Carlisle
F	Forest and Fens	**R**	Reading
G	Garden of England	**S**	Scotland
H	Hampshire and	**T**	Scotland*
	Dorset	**V**	Severn Valley
K	Luton, N W London	**W**	West of England
	and Northampton	**Y**	Yorkshire

The **FIRST TWO LETTERS (two-letter code)** show in which locality or area the mark was issued (see pages 8 to 13), e.g. **AF**06 JXN issued in the Peterborough area. Note, however, that these letters may not have any geographical significance if the mark is cherished (see page 42).

All marks beginning J, T (except TF07, TJ07, TK07 and TN07), U, XG to XY are cherished and have been acquired directly from the DVLA (see page 41).

FO, FU, MN, NF and combinations with letters I, Q or Z are not issued.

*TF07, TJ07, TK07 and TN07 only.

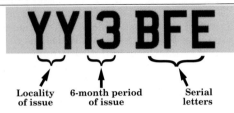

Locality   6-month period   Serial
of issue   of issue   letters

The **DIGITS** (numbers) show in which six-monthly period the
mark was issued.

51	September 2001 to February 2002
02	March to August 2002
52	September 2002 to February 2003
03	March to August 2003
53	September 2003 to February 2004
04	March to August 2004
54	September 2004 to February 2005
05	March to August 2005
55	September 2005 to February 2006
06	March to August 2006
56	September 2006 to February 2007
07	March to August 2007
57	September 2007 to February 2008
08	March to August 2008
58	September 2008 to February 2009
09	March to August 2009
59	September 2009 to February 2010
10	March to August 2010
60	September 2010 to February 2011
11	March to August 2011
61	September 2011 to February 2012
12	March to August 2012
62	September 2012 to February 2013
13	March to August 2013
63	September 2013 to February 2014

6

14	March to August 2014
64	September 2014 to February 2015
15	March to August 2015
65	September 2015 to February 2016
16	March to August 2016
66	September 2016 to February 2017
17	March to August 2017
67	September 2017 to February 2018
18	March to August 2018
68	September 2018 to February 2019
19	March to August 2019
69	September 2019 to February 2020
20	March to August 2020
70	September 2020 to February 2021
21	March to August 2021
71	September 2021 to February 2022
22	March to August 2022
72	September 2022 to February 2023
23	March to August 2023
73	September 2023 to February 2024
24	March to August 2024
74	September 2024 to February 2025
25	March to August 2025
75	September 2025 to February 2026
26	March to August 2026
76	September 2026 to February 2027, etc.

The **LAST THREE LETTERS (serial letters)** are individual to each vehicle but do not normally have any special meaning. Letters I and Q are not used.

However, there are many cherished (personalised or 'private') marks whose last three letters may spell a word or be the owner's initials, etc. (see page 42).

Code	Area	Code	Area
AA	Peterborough	**BT**	Birmingham
AB	Peterborough	**BU**	Birmingham
AC	Peterborough	**BV**	Birmingham
AD	Peterborough	**BW**	Birmingham
AE	Peterborough	**BX**	Birmingham
AF	Peterborough		
AG	Peterborough	**CA**	Cardiff
AJ	Peterborough	**CE**	Cardiff
AK	Peterborough	**CF**	Cardiff
AM	Peterborough	**CJ**	Cardiff
AN	Peterborough	**CK**	Cardiff
AO	Norwich	**CN**	Cardiff
AP	Norwich	**CP**	Swansea
AR	Norwich	**CT**	Swansea
AT	Norwich	**CU**	Swansea
AU	Norwich	**CV**	Swansea
AV	Ipswich	**CW**	Bangor
AW	Ipswich	**CX**	Bangor
AX	Ipswich	**CY**	Bangor
AY	Ipswich		
		DA	Chester
BA	Birmingham	**DC**	Chester
BC	Birmingham	**DE**	Chester
BD	Birmingham	**DF**	Chester
BF	Birmingham	**DG**	Chester
BG	Birmingham	**DK**	Chester
BJ	Birmingham	**DL**	Shrewsbury
BK	Birmingham	**DN**	Shrewsbury
BL	Birmingham	**DP**	Shrewsbury
BM	Birmingham	**DS**	Shrewsbury
BN	Birmingham	**DT**	Shrewsbury
BO	Birmingham	**DU**	Shrewsbury
BP	Birmingham	**DV**	Shrewsbury

Codes not listed (e.g. DR) are likely to be cherished, see page 42.

Code	Area	Code	Area
DX	Shrewsbury	**FY**	Lincoln
DY	Shrewsbury		
		GC	Maidstone
EA	Chelmsford	**GD**	Maidstone
EF	Chelmsford	**GF**	Maidstone
EG	Chelmsford	**GJ**	Maidstone
EJ	Chelmsford	**GK**	Maidstone
EK	Chelmsford	**GL**	Maidstone
EN	Chelmsford	**GM**	Maidstone
EO	Chelmsford	**GN**	Maidstone
EP	Chelmsford	**GP**	Brighton
ET	Chelmsford	**GR**	Brighton
EU	Chelmsford	**GU**	Brighton
EX	Chelmsford	**GV**	Brighton
EY	Chelmsford	**GW**	Brighton
		GX	Brighton
FA	Nottingham	**GY**	Brighton
FB	Nottingham		
FC	Nottingham	**HC**	Bournemouth
FD	Nottingham	**HD**	Bournemouth
FE	Nottingham	**HF**	Bournemouth
FG	Nottingham	**HG**	Bournemouth
FH	Nottingham	**HJ**	Bournemouth
FJ	Nottingham	**HK**	Portsmouth
FL	Nottingham	**HN**	Portsmouth
FM	Nottingham	**HS**	Portsmouth
FN	Nottingham	**HT**	Portsmouth
FP	Nottingham	**HV**	Portsmouth
FR	Lincoln	**HW**	Isle of Wight
FT	Lincoln	**HX**	Portsmouth
FV	Lincoln	**HY**	Portsmouth
FW	Lincoln		
FX	Lincoln		

Codes not listed (e.g. GO) are likely to be cherished, see page 42.

Code	Area	Code	Area
KA	Luton†	**LH**	South West London
KB	Luton†	**LJ**	South West London
KC	Luton†	**LK**	North West London
KD	Luton†	**LL**	North West London
KE	North West London*	**LM**	North West London
KF	North West London*	**LN**	North West London
KG	Luton†	**LO**	North West London
KH	Luton†	**LP**	North West London
KJ	Northampton*	**LR**	North West London
KK	Northampton*	**LS**	North West London
KL	Northampton*	**LT**	North West London
KM	Northampton	**LU**	South East London
KN	Northampton	**LV**	South East London
KO	Northampton	**LW**	South East London
KP	Northampton	**LX**	South East London
KR	Northampton	**LY**	South East London
KS	Northampton		
KT	Northampton	**MA**	Manchester
KU	Northampton	**MC**	Manchester
KV	Northampton	**MD**	Manchester
KW	Northampton	**MF**	Manchester
KX	Northampton	**MH**	Manchester
KY	Northampton	**MJ**	Manchester
		MK	Manchester
LA	South West London	**ML**	Manchester
LB	South West London	**MM**	Manchester
LC	South West London	**MT**	Manchester
LD	South West London	**MU**	Manchester
LE	South West London	**MV**	Manchester
LF	South West London	**MW**	Manchester
LG	South West London	**MX**	Manchester

†Until February 2008 only. *Luton until closure in February 2008.
Codes not listed (e.g. MB) are likely to be cherished, see page 42.

Code	Area	Code	Area
NA	Newcastle	**PO**	Preston
NB	Newcastle	**PV**	Carlisle
NC	Newcastle	**PX**	Carlisle
ND	Newcastle	**PY**	Carlisle
NG	Newcastle		
NH	Newcastle	**RA**	Reading
NJ	Newcastle	**RD**	Reading
NK	Newcastle	**RE**	Reading
NL	Newcastle	**RF**	Reading
NM	Newcastle	**RG**	Reading
NR	Middlesbrough	**RJ**	Reading
NT	Middlesbrough	**RK**	Reading
NU	Middlesbrough	**RL**	Reading
NV	Middlesbrough	**RN**	Reading
NX	Middlesbrough	**RO**	Reading
NY	Middlesbrough	**RV**	Reading
		RX	Reading
OE	Oxford	**RY**	Reading
OU	Oxford		
OV	Oxford	**SA**	Glasgow
OW	Oxford	**SB**	Glasgow
OX	Oxford	**SC**	Glasgow
OY	Oxford	**SD**	Glasgow
		SE	Glasgow
PA	Preston	**SF**	Glasgow
PE	Preston	**SG**	Glasgow
PF	Preston	**SH**	Glasgow
PG	Preston	**SJ**	Glasgow
PJ	Preston	**SK**	Edinburgh
PK	Preston	**SL**	Edinburgh
PL	Preston	**SM**	Edinburgh
PM	Preston	**SN**	Edinburgh
PN	Preston	**SO**	Edinburgh

Codes not listed (e.g. OO) are likely to be cherished, see page 42.

Code	Area	Code	Area
SP	Dundee	**VT**	Worcester
SR	Dundee	**VU**	Worcester
SS	Dundee	**VX**	Worcester
ST	Dundee		
SU	Aberdeen	**WA**	Exeter
SV	Aberdeen	**WD**	Exeter
SW	Aberdeen	**WF**	Exeter
SX	Inverness	**WG**	Exeter
SY	Inverness	**WH**	Exeter
		WJ	Exeter
TF	Glasgow*	**WK**	Truro
TJ	Glasgow*	**WL**	Truro
TK	Edinburgh*	**WM**	Bristol
TN	Edinburgh*	**WN**	Bristol
		WO	Bristol
VA	Worcester	**WP**	Bristol
VE	Worcester	**WR**	Bristol
VF	Worcester	**WT**	Bristol
VK	Worcester	**WU**	Bristol
VN	Worcester	**WV**	Bristol
VO	Worcester	**WX**	Bristol

*TF07, TJ07, TK07 and TN07 only, issued because of a shortage of 'S' marks.
Codes not listed (e.g. VW) are likely to be cherished, see page 42.

Code	When issued
XA	March, September
XB	April, October
XC	May, November
XD	June, December
XE	July, January
XF	August, February

XA-XF issued for VAT-exempt
export vehicles, e.g.
X**D**14 AJT = **June** 2014

Code	Area
YA	Leeds
YB	Leeds
YC	Leeds
YD	Leeds

Code	Area
YE	Leeds
YF	Leeds
YG	Leeds
YH	Leeds
YJ	Leeds
YK	Leeds
YL	Leeds
YM	Sheffield
YN	Sheffield
YO	Sheffield
YP	Sheffield
YR	Sheffield
YS	Sheffield
YT	Sheffield
YU	Sheffield
YV	Sheffield
YW	Hull
YX	Hull
YY	Hull

```
0123456789
ABCDEFGHJKLMN
OPQRSTUVWXYZ
```

*The official font (style of lettering) which must be used
on all current-style number plates.*

Before September 2001 registration marks were based on a scheme begun in 1903. Each county or county borough issued one or more single or double letter codes, e.g. **FM** was issued by Chester Borough Council. Vehicles were numbered from 1 to 9999, e.g. Chester issued **FM** 1 to **FM** 9999. Number plates were black with white or silver characters (letters and numbers).

From 1932 onwards a three-letter system was introduced. The first letter was a 'serial' and the last two letters signified the place of issue. Vehicles were numbered from 1 to 999, e.g. after **FM** 9999 Chester issued A**FM** 1 to A**FM** 999, then B**FM** 1 to B**FM** 999, etc. until Y**FM** 999. Serial letters I, Q and Z were not used in Great Britain, but I is used in Northern Ireland, and I and Z were used in the Irish Republic.

This system was reversed from 1953 onwards with numbers first and one, two or three letters next, e.g. after Y**FM** 999 Chester issued 1 A**FM** to 999 A**FM**, etc.

In 1963 'year letters' were introduced. The original three-letter system was re-started but with a SUFFIX letter at the end signifying the year of issue, e.g. Chester **AFM 1B**, etc. The system was reversed in 1983/4 with a PREFIX year letter at the beginning, e.g. **A21 AFM**, etc. (A1-20 were withheld for future sale as cherished marks.)

Meanwhile, in 1974, issuing of registration marks was transferred from counties and county boroughs to Local Vehicle Licensing Offices, later called DVLA Local Offices, e.g. code **FM** was transferred to Chester LVLO. Number plates on vehicles registered from 1973 onwards were reflective (white front, yellow rear) with black characters.

Suffix and prefix letters are on pages 16 and 17.

Between 1963 and 1983, registration marks were issued with a **suffix** (a letter at the end) which shows the year they were issued.

A	1963
B	1964
C	1965
D	1966
E	January to July 1967
F	August 1967 to July 1968
G	August 1968 to July 1969
H	August 1969 to July 1970
J	August 1970 to July 1971
K	August 1971 to July 1972
L	August 1972 to July 1973
M	August 1973 to July 1974
N	August 1974 to July 1975
P	August 1975 to July 1976
R	August 1976 to July 1977
S	August 1977 to July 1978
T	August 1978 to July 1979
V	August 1979 to July 1980
W	August 1980 to July 1981
X	August 1981 to July 1982
Y	August 1982 to July 1983

The last two letters of the three-letter group show where the mark was issued (e.g. **RVJ** 724S was issued in Hereford).

To find out where suffixed registration marks were issued, see pages 18 to 24.

Between 1983 and 2001, registration marks included a **prefix** (a single letter at the beginning) which shows when they were issued.

A	August 1983 to July 1984
B	August 1984 to July 1985
C	August 1985 to July 1986
D	August 1986 to July 1987
E	August 1987 to July 1988
F	August 1988 to July 1989
G	August 1989 to July 1990
H	August 1990 to July 1991
J	August 1991 to July 1992
K	August 1992 to July 1993
L	August 1993 to July 1994
M	August 1994 to July 1995
N	August 1995 to July 1996
P	August 1996 to July 1997
Q	See page 27
R	August 1997 to July 1998
S	August 1998 to February 1999
T	March to August 1999
V	September 1999 to February 2000
W	March to August 2000
X	September 2000 to February 2001
Y	March to August 2001

The last two letters of a prefixed mark show where the mark was issued (e.g. T698 **SAE** issued in Bristol). To find out where prefixed registration marks were issued, see pages 18 to 24.

Some prefixed marks, including all those with numbers 1 to 20, e.g. **M6** WST, are issued by DVLA as cherished marks (see page 43). Their last two letters do not signify the place of issue.

	Until 1974	*1974 onwards*		*Until 1974*	*1974 onwards*
A	London		**C**	Yorkshire(WR)	
AA	Hampshire	Salisbury +	**CA**	Denbighshire	Chester
AB	Worcestershire	Worcester	**CB**	Blackburn	Bolton +
AC	Warwickshire	Coventry +	**CC**	Caernarvonshire	Bangor
AD	Gloucestershire	Gloucester +	**CD**	Brighton	Brighton
AE	Bristol	Bristol	**CE**	Cambridgeshire	Cambridge +
AF	Cornwall	Truro	**CF**	West Suffolk	Reading
AG	Ayrshire	Hull +	**CG**	Hampshire	Salisbury +
AH	Norfolk	Norwich	**CH**	Derby	Nottingham
AI	Meath	Meath	**CI**	Laois	Laois
AJ	Yorkshire (NR)	Middlesbrough +	**CJ**	Herefordshire	Hereford +
AK	Bradford	Sheffield	**CK**	Preston	Preston
AL	Notts	Nottingham	**CL**	Norwich	Norwich
AM	Wiltshire	Swindon +	**CM**	Birkenhead	Liverpool +
AN	West Ham	Reading	**CN**	Gateshead	Newcastle
	MAN used by Isle of Man		**CO**	Plymouth	Plymouth +
AO	Cumberland	Carlisle	**CP**	Halifax	Huddersfield +
AP	East Sussex	Brighton	**CR**	Southampton	Portsmouth
AR	Hertfordshire	Chelmsford	**CS**	Ayrshire	Ayr +
AS	Nairnshire	Inverness	**CT**	Lincs(Kesteven)	Boston +
AT	Hull	Hull +	**CU**	South Shields	Newcastle
AU	Nottingham	Nottingham	**CV**	Cornwall	Truro
AV	Aberdeenshire	Peterborough	**CW**	Burnley	Preston
AW	Shropshire	Shrewsbury	**CX**	Huddersfield	Huddersfield +
AX	Monmouths.	Cardiff	**CY**	Swansea	Swansea
AY	Leicestershire	Leicester +		*SCY transferred to Cornwall*	
AZ	Belfast	Belfast		*in 1971 for use in Isles of*	
				Scilly.	
			CZ	Belfast	Belfast
B	Lancashire		**D**	Kent	
BA	Salford	Manchester	**DA**	Wolverhampton	Birmingham
BB	Newcastle	Newcastle	**DB**	Stockport	Manchester
BC	Leicester	Leicester +	**DC**	Middlesbrough	Middlesbrough
BD	Northants	Northampton	**DD**	Gloucestershire	Gloucester +
BE	Lincs(Lindsey)	Grimsby +	**DE**	Pembrokeshire	Haverfordwest +
BF	Staffordshire	Stoke-on-Trent +	**DF**	Gloucestershire	Gloucester +
BG	Birkenhead	Liverpool +	**DG**	Gloucestershire	Gloucester +
BH	Bucks	Luton	**DH**	Walsall	Dudley +
BI	Monaghan	Monaghan	**DI**	Roscommon	Roscommon
BJ	East Suffolk	Ipswich	**DJ**	St Helens	Warrington +
BK	Portsmouth	Portsmouth	**DK**	Rochdale	Bolton +
BL	Berkshire	Reading	**DL**	Isle of Wight	Newport(IoW) +
BM	Bedfordshire	Luton	**DM**	Flintshire	Chester
BN	Bolton	Bolton +	**DN**	York	York +
BO	Cardiff	Cardiff	**DO**	Lincs(Holland)	Boston +
BP	West Sussex	Portsmouth	**DP**	Reading	Reading
BR	Sunderland	Durham +	**DR**	Plymouth	Plymouth +
BS	Orkney	Kirkwall +	**DS**	Peeblesshire	Glasgow
BT	Yorkshire(ER)	York +	**DT**	Doncaster	Sheffield
BU	Oldham	Manchester	**DU**	Coventry	Coventry +
BV	Blackburn	Preston	**DV**	Devon	Exeter
BW	Oxfordshire	Oxford	**DW**	Newport(Wales)	Cardiff
BX	Carmarthens.	Haverfordwest +	**DX**	Ipswich	Ipswich
BY	Croydon	London (NW) +	**DY**	Hastings	Hastings +
BZ	Down	Downpatrick	**DZ**	Antrim	Ballymena

+ Office closed, relocated or renamed. See page 25.

	Until 1974	1974 onwards		Until 1974	1974 onwards
E	Staffordshire		FM	Chester	Chester
EA	West Bromwich	Dudley +	FN	Canterbury	Canterbury +
EB	Isle of Ely	Cambridge +	FO	Radnorshire	Hereford +
EC	Westmorland	Kendal +	FP	Rutland	Leicester +
ED	Warrington	Warrington +	FR	Blackpool	Preston
EE	Grimsby	Grimsby +	FS	Edinburgh	Edinburgh
EF	W. Hartlepool	Middlesbrough +	FT	Tynemouth	Newcastle
EG	Peterborough	Peterborough	FU	Lincs(Lindsey)	Grimsby +
EH	Stoke-on-Trent	Stoke-on-Trent +	FV	Blackpool	Preston
EI	Sligo	Sligo	FW	Lincs(Lindsey)	Lincoln
EJ	Cardiganshire	Aberystwyth +	FX	Dorset	Bournemouth
EK	Wigan	Warrington +	FY	Southport	Liverpool +
EL	Bournemouth	Bournemouth	FZ	Belfast	Belfast
EM	Bootle	Liverpool +			
EN	Bury	Bolton +	G	Glasgow	
EO	Barrow	Barrow +	GA	Glasgow	Glasgow
EP	Montgomerys.	Swansea	GB	Glasgow	Glasgow
ER	Cambridgeshire	Cambridge +	GC	London	London SW +
ES	Perthshire	Dundee	GD	Glasgow	Glasgow
ET	Rotherham	Sheffield	GE	Glasgow	Glasgow
EU	Breconshire	Bristol	GF	London	London SW +
EV	Essex	Chelmsford	GG	Glasgow	Glasgow
EW	Huntingdons.	Peterborough	GH	London	London SW +
EX	Gt Yarmouth	Norwich	GI	Tipperary(SR)	Tipperary(SR)
EY	Anglesey	Bangor	GJ	London	London SW +
EZ	Belfast	Belfast	GK	London	London SW +
			GL	Bath	Truro
F	Essex		GM	Motherwell	Reading
FA	Burton-on-Trent	Stoke-on-Trent +	GN	London	London SW +
FB	Bath	Bristol	GO	London	London SW +
FC	Oxford	Oxford	GP	London	London SW +
FD	Dudley	Dudley +	GR	Sunderland	Durham +
FE	Lincoln	Lincoln	GS	Perthshire	Luton
FF	Merionethshire	Aberystwyth +	GT	London	London SW +
FG	Fife	Brighton	GU	London	London SE +
FH	Gloucester	Gloucester +	GV	West Suffolk	Ipswich
FI	Tipperary(NR)	Tipperary(NR)	GW	London	London SE +
FJ	Exeter	Exeter	GX	London	London SE +
FK	Worcester	Dudley +	GY	London	London SE +
FL	Peterborough	Peterborough	GZ	Belfast	Belfast

+ Office closed, relocated or renamed. See page 25.

	Until 1974	*1974 onwards*		*Until 1974*	*1974 onwards*
H	Middlesex		**J**	Durham**	
HA	Smethwick	Dudley +	**JA**	Stockport	Manchester
HB	Merthyr Tydfil	Cardiff	**JB**	Berkshire	Reading
HC	Eastbourne	Hastings +	**JC**	Caernarvonshire	Bangor
HD	Dewsbury	Huddersfield +	**JD**	West Ham	London Central -
HE	Barnsley	Sheffield	**JE**	Isle of Ely	Cambridge +
HF	Wallasey	Liverpool +	**JF**	Leicester	Leicester +
HG	Burnley	Preston	**JG**	Canterbury	Canterbury +
HH	Carlisle	Carlisle	**JH**	Hertfordshire	Reading
HI	Tipperary(SR)	Tipperary(SR)	**JI**	Tyrone	Omagh
HJ	Southend	Chelmsford	**JJ**	London	Canterbury +
HK	Essex	Chelmsford	**JK**	Eastbourne	Hastings +
HL	Wakefield	Sheffield	**JL**	Lincs(Holland)	Boston +
HM	East Ham	London Central +	**JM**	Westmorland	Reading
HN	Darlington	Middlesbrough +	**JN**	Southend	Chelmsford
HO	Hampshire	Salisbury +	**JO**	Oxford	Oxford
HP	Coventry	Coventry +	**JP**	Wigan	Warrington +
HR	Wiltshire	Swindon +	**JR**	Northumberland	Newcastle
HS	Renfrewshire	Glasgow	**JS**	Ross & Cromarty	Stornoway +
HT	Bristol	Bristol	**JT**	Dorset	Bournemouth
HU	Bristol	Bristol	**JU**	Leicestershire	Leicester +
HV	East Ham	London Central +	**JV**	Grimsby	Grimsby +
HW	Bristol	Bristol	**JW**	Wolverhampton	Birmingham
HX	Middlesex	London Central +	**JX**	Halifax	Huddersfield +
HY	Bristol	Bristol	**JY**	Plymouth	Plymouth +
HZ	Tyrone	Omagh	**JZ**	Down	Downpatrick
IA	Antrim	Ballymena	**K**	Liverpool	
IB	Armagh	Armagh	**KA**	Liverpool	Liverpool +
IC	Carlow	Carlow	**KB**	Liverpool	Liverpool +
ID	Cavan	Cavan	**KC**	Liverpool	Liverpool +
IE	Clare	Clare	**KD**	Liverpool	Liverpool +
IF	Cork	Cork	**KE**	Kent	Maidstone
IG	–	Enniskillen	**KF**	Liverpool	Liverpool +
IH	Donegal	Donegal	**KG**	Cardiff	Cardiff
IJ	Down	Downpatrick	**KH**	Hull	Hull +
IK	Dublin	Dublin	**KI**	Waterford	Waterford
IL	Fermanagh	Enniskillen	**KJ**	Kent	Maidstone
IM	Galway	Galway	**KK**	Kent	Maidstone
IN	Kerry	Kerry	**KL**	Kent	Maidstone
IO	Kildare	Kildare	**KM**	Kent	Maidstone
IP	Kilkenny	Kilkenny	**KN**	Kent	Maidstone
IR	Offaly	Offaly	**KO**	Kent	Maidstone
IS	Mayo	Mayo	**KP**	Kent	Maidstone
IT	Leitrim	Leitrim	**KR**	Kent	Maidstone
IU	Limerick	Limerick	**KS**	Roxburghshire	Selkirk +
IV	Limerick	Limerick	**KT**	Kent	Canterbury +
IW	Londonderry	Coleraine	**KU**	Bradford	Sheffield
IX	Longford	Longford	**KV**	Coventry	Coventry +
IY	Louth	Louth	**KW**	Bradford	Sheffield
IZ	Mayo	Mayo	**KX**	Bucks	Luton
			KY	Bradford	Sheffield
			KZ	Antrim	Ballymena

**Most single J marks now seen in the U.K. are registered in Jersey. See page 28.

+ Office closed, relocated or renamed. See page 25.

	Until 1974	1974 onwards			Until 1974	1974 onwards
L	Glamorgans.		**N**		Manchester	
LA	London	London NW +	**NA**		Manchester	Manchester
LB	London	London NW +	**NB**		Manchester	Manchester
LC	London	London NW +	**NC**		Manchester	Manchester
LD	London	London NW +	**ND**		Manchester	Manchester
LE	London	London NW +	**NE**		Manchester	Manchester
LF	London	London NW +	**NF**		Manchester	Manchester
LG	Cheshire	Chester	**NG**		Norfolk	Norwich
LH	London	London NW +	**NH**		Northampton	Northampton
LI	Westmeath	Westmeath	**NI**		Wicklow	Wicklow
LJ	Bournemouth	Bournemouth			QNI issued in Northern	
LK	London	London NW +			Ireland, see page 26.	
LL	London	London NW +	**NJ**		East Sussex	Brighton
LM	London	London NW +	**NK**		Hertfordshire	Luton
LN	London	London NW +	**NL**		Northumberland	Newcastle
LO	London	London NW +	**NM**		Bedfordshire	Luton
LP	London	London NW +	**NN**		Notts	Nottingham
LR	London	London NW +	**NO**		Essex	Chelmsford
LS	Selkirkshire	Stirling +	**NP**		Worcestershire	Worcester
LT	London	London NW +	**NR**		Leicestershire	Leicester +
LU	London	London NW +	**NS**		Sutherland	Glasgow
LV	Liverpool	Liverpool +	**NT**		Shropshire	Shrewsbury
LW	London	London NW +	**NU**		Derbyshire	Nottingham
LX	London	London NW +	**NV**		Northants	Northampton
LY	London	London NW +	**NW**		Leeds	Leeds
LZ	Armagh	Armagh	**NX**		Warwickshire	Dudley +
			NY		Glamorganshire	Cardiff
			NZ		Londonderry	Coleraine
M	Cheshire		**O**		Birmingham	
MA	Cheshire	Chester	**OA**		Birmingham	Birmingham
MB	Cheshire	Chester	**OB**		Birmingham	Birmingham
MC	Middlesex	London NE +	**OC**		Birmingham	Birmingham
MD	Middlesex	London NE +	**OD**		Devon	Exeter
ME	Middlesex	London NE +	**OE**		Birmingham	Birmingham
MF	Middlesex	London NE +	**OF**		Birmingham	Birmingham
MG	Middlesex	London NE +	**OG**		Birmingham	Birmingham
MH	Middlesex	London NE +	**OH**		Birmingham	Birmingham
MI	Wexford	Wexford	**OI**		Belfast	Belfast
MJ	Bedfordshire	Luton	**OJ**		Birmingham	Birmingham
MK	Middlesex	London NE +	**OK**		Birmingham	Birmingham
ML	Middlesex	London NE +	**OL**		Birmingham	Birmingham
MM	Middlesex	London NE +	**OM**		Birmingham	Birmingham
MN	Isle of Man	Isle of Man	**ON**		Birmingham	Birmingham
MO	Berkshire	Reading	**OO**		Essex	Chelmsford
MP	Middlesex	London NE +	**OP**		Birmingham	Birmingham
MR	Wiltshire	Swindon +	**OR**		Hampshire	Portsmouth
MS	Stirlingshire	Stirling +	**OS**		Wigtownshire	Stranraer +
MT	Middlesex	London NE +	**OT**		Hampshire	Portsmouth
MU	Middlesex	London NE +	**OU**		Hampshire	Bristol
MV	Middlesex	London SE +	**OV**		Birmingham	Birmingham
MW	Wiltshire	Swindon +	**OW**		Southampton	Portsmouth
MX	Middlesex	London SE +	**OX**		Birmingham	Birmingham
MY	Middlesex	London SE +	**OY**		Croydon	London NW +
MZ	Belfast	Belfast	**OZ**		Belfast	Belfast

+ Office closed, relocated or renamed. See page 25.

	Until 1974	*1974 onwards*		*Until 1974*	*1974 onwards*
P	Surrey		RL	Cornwall	Truro
PA	Surrey	Guildford +	RM	Cumberland	Carlisle
PB	Surrey	Guildford +	RN	Preston	Preston
PC	Surrey	Guildford +	RO	Hertfordshire	Luton
PD	Surrey	Guildford +	RP	Northants.	Northampton
PE	Surrey	Guildford +	RR	Notts.	Nottingham
PF	Surrey	Guildford +	RS	Aberdeen	Aberdeen
PG	Surrey	Guildford +	RT	East Suffolk	Ipswich
PH	Surrey	Guildford +	RU	Bournemouth	Bournemouth
PI	Cork	Cork	RV	Portsmouth	Portsmouth
PJ	Surrey	Guildford +	RW	Coventry	Coventry +
PK	Surrey	Guildford +	RX	Berkshire	Reading
PL	Surrey	Guildford +	RY	Leicester	Leicester +
PM	East Sussex	Guildford +	RZ	Antrim	Ballymena
PN	East Sussex	Brighton			
PO	West Sussex	Portsmouth	S	Edinburgh	
	GPO issued by London CC		SA	Aberdeenshire	Aberdeen
	for General Post Office		SB	Argyllshire	Oban +
PP	Bucks.	Luton	SC	Edinburgh	Edinburgh
PR	Dorset	Bournemouth	SD	Ayrshire	Ayr +
PS	Shetland	Lerwick +	SE	Banff	Keith +
PT	Durham	Durham +	SF	Edinburgh	Edinburgh
PU	Essex	Chelmsford	SG	Edinburgh	Edinburgh
PV	Ipswich	Ipswich	SH	Berwickshire	Selkirk +
PW	Norfolk	Norwich	SI	Dublin	Dublin
PX	West Sussex	Portsmouth	SJ	Bute	Ayr +
PY	Yorkshire (NR)	Middlesbrough +	SK	Caithness	Wick +
PZ	Belfast	Belfast	SL	Clackmannans.	Dundee
			SM	Dumfriesshire	Dumfries +
R	Derbyshire		SN	Dunbartonshire	Dundee
RA	Derbyshire	Nottingham	SO	Moray	Aberdeen
RB	Derbyshire	Nottingham	SP	Fife	Dundee
RC	Derby	Nottingham	SR	Angus	Dundee
RD	Reading	Reading	SS	East Lothian	Aberdeen
RE	Staffordshire	Stoke-on-Trent +	ST	Invernessshire	Inverness
RF	Staffordshire	Stoke-on-Trent +	SU	Kincardineshire	Glasgow
RG	Aberdeen	Newcastle	SV	Kinrossshire	–
RH	Hull	Hull +	SW	Kirkcudbrights.	Dumfries +
RI	Dublin	Dublin	SX	West Lothian	Edinburgh
RJ	Salford	Manchester	SY	Midlothian	–
RK	Croydon	London NW +	SZ	Down	Downpatrick

QA to **QY** were issued (pre-1974) by London County Council, AA and RAC; and (1974 onwards) by London Central (+) for vehicles temporarily imported from abroad.

+ Office closed, relocated or renamed. See page 25.

	Until 1974	1974 onwards		Until 1974	1974 onwards
T	Devon		V	Lanarkshire	
TA	Devon	Exeter	VA	Lanarkshire	Cambridge +
TB	Lancashire	Warrington +	VB	Croydon	Canterbury +
TC	Lancashire	Bristol	VC	Coventry	Coventry +
TD	Lancashire	Bolton +	VD	Lanarkshire	Luton
TE	Lancashire	Bolton +	VE	Cambridgeshire	Cambridge +
TF	Lancashire	Reading	VF	Norfolk	Norwich
TG	Glamorgans.	Cardiff	VG	Norwich	Norwich
TH	Carmarthens.	Swansea	VH	Huddersfield	Huddersfield +
TI	Limerick	Limerick	VJ	Herefordshire	Hereford +
TJ	Lancashire	Liverpool +	VK	Newcastle	Newcastle
TK	Dorset	Plymouth +	VL	Lincoln	Lincoln
TL	Lincs(Kesteven)	Lincoln	VM	Manchester	Manchester
TM	Bedfordshire	Luton	VN	Yorkshire(NR)	Middlesbrough +
TN	Newcastle	Newcastle	VO	Notts.	Nottingham
TO	Nottingham	Nottingham	VP	Birmingham	Birmingham
TP	Portsmouth	Portsmouth	VR	Manchester	Manchester
TR	Southampton	Portsmouth	VS	Greenock	Luton
TS	Dundee	Dundee	VT	Stoke-on-Trent	Stoke-on-Trent +
TT	Devon	Exeter	VU	Manchester	Manchester
TU	Cheshire	Chester	VV	Northampton	Northampton
TV	Nottingham	Nottingham	VW	Essex	Chelmsford
TW	Essex	Chelmsford	VX	Essex	Chelmsford
TX	Glamorganshire	Cardiff	VY	York	York +
TY	Northumberland	Newcastle	VZ	Tyrone	Omagh
TZ	Belfast	Belfast			
U	Leeds		W	Sheffield	
UA	Leeds	Leeds	WA	Sheffield	Sheffield
UB	Leeds	Leeds	WB	Sheffield	Sheffield
UC	London	London Central +	WC	Essex	Chelmsford
UD	Oxfordshire	Oxford	WD	Warwickshire	Dudley +
UE	Warwickshire	Dudley +	WE	Sheffield	Sheffield
UF	Brighton	Brighton	WF	Yorkshire(ER)	Sheffield
UG	Leeds	Leeds	WG	Stirlingshire	Sheffield
UH	Cardiff	Cardiff	WH	Bolton	Bolton +
UI	Londonderry	Londonderry	WI	Waterford	Waterford
UJ	Shropshire	Shrewsbury	WJ	Sheffield	Sheffield
UK	Wolverhampton	Birmingham	WK	Coventry	Coventry +
UL	London	London Central +	WL	Oxford	Oxford
UM	Leeds	Leeds	WM	Southport	Liverpool +
UN	Denbighshire	Barnstaple +	WN	Swansea	Swansea
UO	Devon	Barnstaple +	WO	Monmouthshire	Cardiff
UP	Durham	Durham +	WP	Worcestershire	Worcester
UR	Hertfordshire	Luton	WR	Yorkshire(WR)	Leeds
US	Glasgow	Glasgow	WS	Edinburgh	Bristol
UT	Leicestershire	Leicester +	WT	Yorkshire(WR)	Leeds
UU	London	London Central +	WU	Yorkshire(WR)	Leeds
UV	London	London Central +	WV	Wiltshire	Brighton
UW	London	London Central +	WW	Yorkshire(WR)	Leeds
UX	Shropshire	Shrewsbury	WX	Yorkshire(WR)	Leeds
UY	Worcestershire	Worcester	WY	Yorkshire(WR)	Leeds
UZ	Belfast	Belfast	WZ	Belfast	Belfast

+ Office closed, relocated or renamed. See page 25.

	Until 1974	1974 onwards
X	Northumberland	
XA	London	
	Kirkcaldy 1963 on	–
XB	London	
	Coatbridge 1963 on	–
XC	London	
	Solihull 1964 on	–
XD	London	
	Luton 1964 on	–
XE	London	
	Luton 1964 on	–
XF	London	
	Torbay 1968 on	–
XG	Middlesbrough	–
XH	London	–
XI	Belfast	Belfast
XJ	Manchester	–
XK	London	–
XL	London	–
XM	London	–
XN	London	–
XO	London	–
XP	London	Temporary registrations for export vehicles
XR	London	–
XS	Paisley	London Central + RXS only. Used for some diplomats' cars.
XT	London	–
XU	London	–
XV	London	–
XW	London	–
XX	London	–
XY	London	–
XZ	Armagh	Armagh
Y	Somerset	
YA	Somerset	Taunton +
YB	Somerset	Taunton +
YC	Somerset	Taunton +
YD	Somerset	Taunton +
YE	London	London Central +
YF	London	London Central +
YG	Yorkshire(WR)	Leeds
YH	London	London Central +
YI	Dublin	Dublin

	Until 1974	1974 onwards
YJ	Dundee	Brighton
YK	London	London Central +
YL	London	London Central +
YM	London	London Central +
YN	London	London Central +
YO	London	London Central +
YP	London	London Central +
YR	London	London Central +
YS	Glasgow	Glasgow
YT	London	London Central +
YU	London	London Central +
YV	London	London Central +
YW	London	London Central +
YX	London	London Central +
YY	London	London Central +
YZ	Londonderry	Coleraine
Z	Dublin	
ZA	Dublin	Dublin
ZB	Cork	Cork
ZC	Dublin	Dublin
ZD	Dublin	Dublin
ZE	Dublin	Dublin
ZF	Cork	Cork
ZG	Dublin	Dublin
ZH	Dublin	Dublin
ZI	Dublin	Dublin
ZJ	Dublin	Dublin
ZK	Cork	Cork
ZL	Dublin	Dublin
ZM	Galway	Galway
ZN	Meath	Meath
ZO	Dublin	Dublin
ZP	Donegal	Donegal
ZR	Wexford	Wexford
ZS	Dublin	Dublin
ZT	Cork	Cork
ZU	Dublin	Dublin
ZV	Dublin	Dublin
	AZV to YZV only. ZV without prefix used as 'age-related' marks for old vehicles.	
ZW	Kildare	Kildare
ZX	Kerry	Kerry
ZY	Louth	Louth
ZZ	Dublin and other offices for temporary imports.	

+ Office closed, relocated or renamed. See opposite page.

CLOSURE OF LOCAL VEHICLE LICENSING OFFICES 1980-1997

Office	Date	Business transferred to
Aberystwyth	1981	Haverfordwest (until 1996) and Bangor
Ayr	1981	Glasgow
Barnstaple	1981	Exeter
Barrow-in-Furness	1981	Preston
Bolton	1981	Manchester
Boston	1981	Lincoln
Cambridge	1980	Peterborough
Canterbury	1981	Maidstone
Coventry	1997	Birmingham, Northampton, Nottingham, Oxford and Worcester
Dudley	1993	Birmingham
Dumfries	1981	Carlisle
Durham	1981	Newcastle upon Tyne
Gloucester	1997	Bristol and Worcester
Grimsby	1980	Lincoln
Guildford	1997	Portsmouth, Reading and Wimbledon
Hastings	1980	Brighton
Haverfordwest	1997	Swansea
Hereford	1981	Gloucester (until 1997)
Huddersfield	1994	Leeds
Keith	1981	Aberdeen
Kendal	1981	Preston
Kirkwall	1980	Inverness
Leicester	1996	Birmingham, Northampton, Nottingham and Peterborough
Lerwick	1980	Aberdeen
Liverpool	1996	Chester and Preston
London Central	1997	Wimbledon
London NE	1996	Chelmsford
Newport (Isle of Wight)	1981	Portsmouth
Oban	1980	Glasgow
Plymouth	1980	Exeter
Salisbury	1980	Bournemouth
Selkirk	1980	Edinburgh
At Newtown St Boswells until 1975		
Stirling	1981	Edinburgh
Stoke-on-Trent	1996	Birmingham and Shrewsbury
Stornoway	1980	Inverness
Stranraer	1981	Glasgow
Swindon	1997	Bristol
Taunton	1996	Bristol and Exeter
Warrington	1981	Liverpool (until 1996)
Wick	1981	Inverness
York	1980	Leeds

Hull office was relocated to Beverley in 1996.
London NW (later known as Stanmore) was relocated to Borehamwood in 2006.
London SE was later known as Sidcup.
London SW was later known as Wimbledon.
Middlesbrough office was relocated to Stockton-on-Tees in 2000.
Reading office was relocated to Theale in 2007.

All Local Vehicle Licensing Offices were finally closed in 2013.

NORTHERN IRELAND uses the old-style pre-1963 U.K. system with two letters before or after a maximum of four digits, or three letters **followed by** up to **four** digits. All marks contain letter I or letter Z (or both). The last two letters of a three-letter code show the area in which the mark was issued.

AZ	Belfast	**IJ**	Downpatrick	**PZ**	Belfast
BZ	Downpatrick	**IL**	Enniskillen	**RZ**	Ballymena
CZ	Belfast	**IW**	Coleraine	**SZ**	Downpatrick
DZ	Ballymena	**JI**	Omagh	**TZ†**	Belfast
EZ	Belfast	**JZ**	Downpatrick	**UI**	Londonderry
FZ	Belfast	**KZ**	Ballymena	**UZ**	Belfast
GZ	Belfast	**LZ**	Armagh	**VZ**	Omagh
HZ	Omagh	**MZ**	Belfast	**WZ**	Belfast
IA	Ballymena	**NZ**	Coleraine	**XI**	Belfast
IB	Armagh	**OI**	Belfast	**XZ**	Armagh
IG*	Enniskillen	**OZ**	Belfast	**YZ**	Coleraine

QNI is issued in Northern Ireland for vehicles whose date of manufacture is unknown, e.g. kit cars, etc. **ZIA** is issued for VAT-exempt export vehicles.

*With prefix letters only, e.g. FIG. Marks in the two-letter series IG are used as replacements/re-registrations for pre-1975 vehicles, e.g. IG 4099 on a 1971 Ford (see also page 49).

†LTZ 1001 onwards specially allocated to London for the New Routemaster bus series (see page 44).

TRADE PLATES are issued to motor manufacturers, agents and dealers to enable unlicensed or unregistered vehicles to be driven lawfully on the roads. They are used temporarily for test driving new cars, moving vehicles from garage to garage, etc.

Trade plates are white with red characters. A new five-digit format (without letters) was introduced in 2013. Older plates have a three-digit number followed by an old-style code, see pages 18 to 24.

Q PLATES

(a) Registration marks with an old-style Q prefix, e.g. Q129 RMA, are issued for vehicles whose precise age is not known, such as imports, kit cars, or vehicles made up from parts of other vehicles. The last two letters show for which area the mark was issued, see pages 18 to 24 (*1974 onwards column*).

(b) Marks with a central Q, e.g. 522 Q12, are issued for temporarily imported vehicles which are either not required to be registered in their home country or have foreign number plates which contain no western-style letters or digits. The last two digits show the half-year of issue, see pages 6 and 7.

Offshore islands number plates are generally similar to those on mainland UK (white reflective front and yellow reflective rear with black characters, or black with white or silver characters).

JERSEY regular issue registration marks consist of the letter J followed by up to six digits. An additional series consisting of letters JSY followed by up to three digits is also issued, but marks in this series can be obtained only by purchase at auction. Plates are reflective white/yellow as on the mainland but vehicles first registered before 1976 may carry black plates with white or silver characters.

The Jersey government holds an annual registration mark auction offering distinctive J marks (usually with four or fewer digits) and JSY marks. Special marks in the J series with five or six digits are available to purchase directly from the government (current price £250).

Address: Driver and Vehicle Standards, La Route de Veulle, La Collette, St Helier, Jersey JE1 3UE.
Telephone: 01534 448600. Website: www.gov.je

GUERNSEY regular issue marks consist of a number of up to five digits (but no letters). Plates can be reflective white/yellow or black.

Marks beginning with zero (0) or double zero (00), e.g. 0013, 0770, can be purchased at auctions along with other 'special' marks (low numbers, palindromes, etc.).
See www.martelmaidesauctions.com

Address: Vehicle Registration and Licensing Department, PO Box 145, Bulwer Avenue, St Sampsons, Guernsey GY1 3HY.
Telephone: 01481 243400. Website: www.gov.gg

(continued on page 30)

Guernsey   *Jersey, cherished*

Alderney   *Jersey*

Isle of Man

ALDERNEY marks consist of the letters AY followed by up to four digits. Plates can be reflective white/yellow or black.

Address: States Office, PO Box 1001, Alderney GY9 3AA. Telephone: 01481 822811. Website: www.alderney.gov.gg

ISLE OF MAN marks contain various combinations of MN, MAN and MANX with various series of numbers. Most plates are reflective white/yellow but some are black.

MN and MAN can be preceded or followed by up to four digits, e.g. MN 353, 8646 MAN.

MAN can be preceded or followed by a single-letter prefix or suffix. Unlike Great Britain, the prefix or suffix is a serial letter which does not indicate year of issue. Also unlike Great Britain, letters O and U are used as prefixes and the letter U as a suffix. Letters I, S and Z are not used.

Marks with letters MANX are 'cherished' and can be purchased (along with other Manx marks) online at www. gov.im under Travel, Traffic and Motoring. They can be preceded or followed by up to three digits.

The current normal series began in 1987 and consists of the letters MN preceded by a single letter, followed by up to three digits, followed by a suffix letter (except I, O, S and Z). The suffix is a serial letter which does not indicate the year of issue. Regulation plates (which are not mandatory) have the groups of characters separated by hyphens, e.g. JMN-889-F, and incorporate a left-hand red band with the three-legged Manx emblem and letters GBM.

Address: Department of Infrastructure, Licensing Office, Sea Terminal Building, Douglas, Isle of Man IM1 2RF. Telephone: 01624 686827. Website: www.gov.im

SCILLY ISLES from 1971 to 2001 used SCY marks from J suffix to Y prefix. The marks were issued in Truro.

From 1994 onwards, Army and Royal Air Force vehicles have been issued with Equipment Registration Marks (ERMs) consisting of two letters followed by two digits followed by AA or, since 2003, AB, e.g. MC 67 AA, SL 59 AB.

Before 1939, most military vehicles carried ordinary civilian marks, usually issued by Middlesex County Council. There were exceptions to this rule during World War I. Between 1939 and 1949, vehicles carried War Department numbers – RAF followed by digits for Royal Air Force, digits followed by RN for Royal Navy, and Army serial numbers preceded by a letter denoting type of vehicle, e.g. F for armoured cars. Some of these early numbers may still be seen at military museums and rallies.

For military vehicles registered between 1949 and 1994, marks consist of two digits followed by a two-letter code followed by two digits, e.g. 28 GT 97. The code often has a special meaning as shown below. Some of these codes, notably AY and RN, are still issued.

Basic allocation of marks with middle letter codes is

AA to AZ	- Royal Air Force
BA to HZ	- Army 1949-1983
KA to KM	- Royal Air Force and Army 1982-1994
RN	- Royal Navy

Some special codes are

AY	- Royal Air Force specialist equipment
BT	- Army miscellaneous, including acquisitions from other armed services
CP	- Army construction plant
MH	- Army mechanical handling equipment (fork-lift trucks, etc)
NE	- Royal Navy mechanical handling equipment (fork-lift trucks, etc)
RA to RH	- Army rebuilt vehicles from pre-1949
SP	- Army special project research vehicles
TF	- Army fire pump trailers
TG	- Army mobile guns
TM	- Army trailer-mounted equipment
WA to WB	- Research and development equipment

XA to XK	- Vehicles commissioned in Germany
YA to YZ	- Army renumbered pre-1949 vehicles
ZA to ZC	- Army renumbered pre-1949 vehicles
ZR to ZY	- Army renumbered pre-1949 vehicles

Many military vehicles have black number plates with white characters but others, especially those used for non-tactical purposes, have modern-style white/yellow reflective plates. Some passenger-carrying vehicles and those not used on military bases are issued with ordinary civilian registration marks for security reasons. However, these vehicles, if actually owned by the armed forces and not by outside contractors, are also allocated military marks (ERMs) for internal purposes.

A fuller list of military codes and further military vehicle information can be found in 'A History of Motor Vehicle Registration in the United Kingdom' (see page 79).

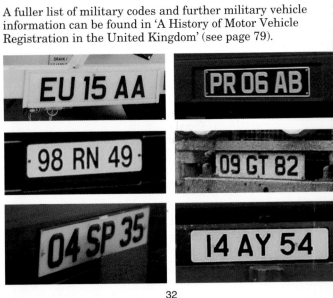

Seen mostly in London and sometimes in other large cities, cars belonging to foreign embassies, commonwealth high commissions, consulates and international organizations have special registration marks.

The official 'flag car' of an ambassador or high commissioner in London usually has a cherished mark which has been specially issued with letters suited to the name of the country, e.g. SVK 1A for the Slovakian ambassador, 1 KEN for the Kenyan high commissioner.

Other diplomatic staff have marks consisting of three digits followed by letter D followed by three digits. Consular or non-diplomatic staff have marks consisting of three digits, letter X and three digits. The first three digits of diplomatic or consular marks show the country or organization, e.g. 256 for Sri Lanka. Three-digit codes beginning with 9 belong to international organizations, e.g. 915 for the International Wheat Council. The digits (but not the letters) on these special plates are usually of a thinner than normal style.

On the following pages the country codes are shown in numerical order with the flag car number, if known, in brackets after the country name. The flag car numbers quoted in the list are based partly on official information and partly on sightings by registration enthusiasts over the past four years.

Marks with codes from 350 to 899 are mostly unidentifiable for security reasons.

The Commonwealth Secretary General's car is registered CSG 1.

101	Afghanistan (1 AFG)	157	Gabon (1 GAB)
102	Algeria (ALG 1A)	158	Gambia (1 GAM)
103	Argentina (1 ARG)	160	Germany (1 GER)
104	Australia (AUS 1)	164	Moldova
105	Australia	165	Ghana (1 GHA)
109	Austria (1 OES)	166	Greece (1 GRC)
110	Bahamas (1 BMS)	168	Grenada
111	Bahrain (BAH 1)	169	Guinea
112	Bangladesh (BDH 1)	170	Guyana (GYA 1)
113	Barbados (BDS 1)	171	Haiti
114	Belgium (1 BE)	172	Honduras
115	Benin	173	Hungary (1 MAG)
116	Bolivia (BOL 1)	174	Iceland (IC 1)
117	Botswana (BOT 1)	175	India (IND 1)
118	Brazil (BRZ 1)	180	Indonesia (RI 1)
123	Bulgaria (BG 1)	181	Iran
124	Myanmar	183	Iraq (1 RAQ)
125	Burundi	184	Cambodia
126	Cameroon (1 CAM)	185	Ireland
127	Canada (CAN 1, CDA 2)	186	Israel
134	Chile (CHI 1)	188	Italy (ITA 1)
135	China (CHN 1)	189	Italy
136	Colombia (COL 1)	191	Côte d'Ivoire (1 RCI)
138	Costa Rica (1 COS)	192	Jamaica (1 JAM)
139	Cuba	193	Japan (JPN 1D)
140	Cyprus (1 CY)	194	Jordan (HKJ 111)
141	Czech Republic (1 CZE)	196	Kenya (1 KEN)
142	Denmark	197	South Korea (1 ROK)
143	Dominican Republic	198	Kuwait (1 KUW)
144	Ecuador (1 ECU)	199	Laos
145	Egypt	200	Lebanon (1 RL)
148	El Salvador (ELS 1)	201	Lesotho (1 LES)
149	Ethiopia (1 EE)	202	Liberia (LEM 1)
150	Fiji	203	North Korea (PRK 1D)
151	Finland (FIN 1)	204	Luxembourg (1 LUX)
153	France (FRA 1)	205	Malawi (1 MLW)
154	France	206	Malaysia (1 M)

208	Malta (1 MLT)	259	Sweden (1 SVE)
209	Mauritania (1 MRN)	260	Switzerland
210	Mauritius (MAU 1)	261	Syria
211	Mexico (MEX 1)	262	Tanzania (1 TAN)
212	Mongolia	263	Thailand (THA 12)
213	Morocco (MOR 1D)	265	Tonga (1 TON)
214	Nepal (NEP 1)	266	Trinidad+Tobago
215	Netherlands (NL 1, NL 2)	267	Tunisia (TUN 1)
218	New Zealand (NZ 1)	268	Turkey
220	Nicaragua (NIC 1)	269	UA Emirates (1 UAE)
222	Nigeria (FGN 1)	274	U S A
225	Norway (1 NWY)	275	Uruguay (1 ROU)
226	Oman (OMA 1N)	276	Venezuela (1 VEN)
227	Pakistan	277	Vietnam (1 VNA)
229	Panama (PAN 1)	278	Yemen (1 YEM)
230	Papua New Guinea (1 PNG)	279	Yemen
231	Paraguay	280	Serbia
232	Peru (PE 1)	281	Congo D Rep (CDR 1)
233	Philippines (PHI 1)	282	Zambia (ZAM 1)
234	Poland (1 POL)	283	Dominica (DOM 1A)
235	Portugal (1 POR)	284	Monaco
236	Qatar (QTR 1)	286	St Lucia (1 SLU)
237	Romania (ROM 1)	287	Uganda (1 UGA)
238	Rwanda (RWA 1A)	289	StVin + Gren (2 SVG)
239	Saudi Arabia	290	Zimbabwe (ZIM 1)
241	Senegal	291	Vatican (1 VCN)
242	Seychelles (SEY 1)	292	East Caribbean
243	Sierra Leone (HSL 1)	293	Belize (BEL 12E)
244	Singapore (SGP 1)	294	Brunei (1 NBD)
245	Somalia	295	Antigua (ANU 1)
246	South Africa (1 RSA)	296	Angola
247	Tajikistan	297	Guatemala
251	Russia (1 RF)	298	Mozambique (1 MOZ)
253	Spain (SPA 1N)	299	Namibia (1 NAM)
256	Sri Lanka (1 SL)	300	Lithuania (1 LIT)
257	Sudan (SUD 1, 2 SUD)	301	Armenia
258	Swaziland (1 SZD)	302	Slovenia (1 SVN)

303 Latvia	314 Eritrea
304 Estonia (1 EST)	315 Kazakhstan (1 KAZ)
305 Croatia (1 HRV)	316 Georgia (1 GRG)
306 Ukraine (UKR 1)	317 Maldives
307 Slovakia (SVK 1A)	318 Turkmenistan (1 TUR)
308 Belarus (1 BLS)	319 Kyrgyzstan
309 Albania	320 St Kitts-Nevis (1 SCN)
310 Azerbaijan	321 Montenegro
311 Macedonia (1 MAK)	324 San Marino
312 Bosnia+Herzeg (BOS 1A)	328 South Sudan
313 Uzbekistan (1 UZB)	330 Kosovo

900 Commonwealth Secretariat
901 Commission of the European Community
902 Council of Europe
903 European Centre for Medium-Range Weather Forecasts
904 European Organisation for the Safety of Air Navigation
905 European Parliament
906 Inter-American Development Bank
907 International Maritime Organization (1 MO)
908 International Cocoa Organization
909 International Coffee Organization
910 International Finance Corporation
911 International Labour Organization
912 International Sugar Organization
913 European Police College
914 International Whaling Commission
915 International Wheat Council

916 North Atlantic Treaty Organization
917 United Nations
918 Western European Union
919 World Health Organization
920 Eastern Caribbean Commission
921 Joint European Torus
922 International Oil Pollution Compensation Fund
923 International Maritime Satellite Organization
924 Commonwealth Foundation
925 International Maritime Organization (Permanent
        Representative)
926 Commonwealth Telecommunications Bureau
927 United Nations High Commissioner for Refugees
928 Commonwealth Agricultural Bureau
929 International Lead and Zinc Corporation
931 Joint European Torus
932 North Atlantic Salmon Conservation Organization
933 European Investment Bank
934 European Telecommunications Satellite Organization
935 European School (Oxford)
936 African Development Bank
937 European Bank for Reconstruction and Development
938 European Bank for Reconstruction and Development
940 European Bioinformatics Institute
941 European Medicines Agency
963 Hong Kong Economic and Trade Office

CIVIC AND OFFICIAL

Many official cars used by mayors, provosts and other senior members of city, town or county councils have cherished marks. These are often very old marks originally issued by the councils or they have letters relating to their names.

The Lord Mayor of London and some Scottish provosts have specially created zero marks, e.g. G 0 for the Lord Provost of Glasgow.

Aberdeen	RG 0	Edinburgh	S 0, S 10,
Argyll & Bute	N100 ABC		SS 10
Barnsley	THE 1	Enfield	M1 ENF
Belfast	1 WZ	Essex	ECC 1
Bexley	H7 BEX	Exeter	1 CFJ
Birmingham	LOM 1	Fareham	T1 FBC
Blackburn	CB 1	Fylde	M4 FBC
Bolton	WH 1	Gateshead	GCN 1
Bournemouth	EL 1	Glasgow	G 0, V 0
Bradford	PKW 1M	Gosport	1 NCG
Brighton & Hove	H2 OVE	Hastings	DY 1066
Bristol	AE 1	Hull	KH 1, 1 KH
Bromley	LBB 1L	Inverclyde	VS 0
Burnley	HG 1	Kensington &	
Bury	T6 BUR	Chelsea	R111 BKC
Camden	CAM 300C	Kingston-upon-	
Charnwood	YUT 1	Thames	RBK 1
Cheshire West		Kirklees	MVH 1
& Chester	TTU 1	Lancaster	L 50
Chesterfield	GVU 1V	Leamington Spa	L100 SPA
Clackmannanshire	SL 1*	Leeds	U 1
Coventry	1 COV	Leicester	ABC 1,
Crawley	H6 CBC		1 ABC
Croydon	1 BY	Lincoln	JFE 1
Derby	CCH 1	London (City)	LM 0
Devon	J1 DCC	Maidstone	1 MKP
Doncaster	KDT 1D	Manchester	N 10
Dundee	TS 1	Merthyr Tydfil	HB 1
East Renfrewshire	HS 0	Midlothian	SY 0

*On loan from the Earl of Mar and Kellie.

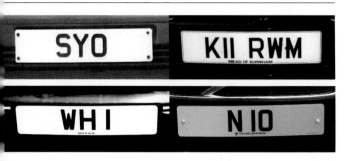

Newcastle upon Tyne	OBB 1	Scarborough	XVN 1,
Newport	NDW 1		XVN 1K
North East		Slough	MPP 1
Lincolnshire	M100 NEL	Solihull	SOL 1
North Lanarkshire	AXB 1B	South Lanarkshire	R100 SLC
North Lincolnshire	L1 NLC	South Ribble	S11 RBC
Northampton	NH 1	Southend-on-Sea	HJ 1
Nottingham	NTV 1	Stockport	JJA 1
Nuneaton		Stockton-on-Tees	SDC 1M
& Bedworth	NBC 1W	Stoke-on-Trent	1 VT
Oldham	ABU 1	Sunderland	OGR 1
Oxford	FC 1	Walsall	DH 1
Perth & Kinross	ES 1	Warrington	ED 1
Peterborough	EG 1	Westminster	WE 1
Plymouth	HJY 1	Wigan	AEK 1
Poole	APR 1	Windsor	
Portsmouth	BK 1	& Maidenhead	K11 RWM
Preston	CCK 1	Wirral	WCM 1M
Reigate & Banstead	M111 RBC	Woking	H1 WBC
Rochdale	DK 1	Wolverhampton	DA 1, JDA 1
Rotherham	ET 1	Wyre	WBC 74
Rugby	MWD 1	York	DN 1
St Helens	CDJ 1	Yorkshire, E Riding	1 BBB,
Salford	RJ 1		GWF 1
Sandwell	1 EA, 1 HA		

CHERISHED (or personalised, or private) registration marks are those which have a special meaning for the people who use them. The main reasons that marks may be cherished are (a) they contain the owner's initials, or (b) they spell a word or name, or (c) they have been kept by the owner or handed down through the family, or (d) they advertise the owner's business, or (e) the owner wishes to hide the age of the vehicle by using an old (or Northern Ireland) mark which does not include a year identifier.

All kinds of U.K. civilian registration marks may be cherished and most can be transferred from vehicle to vehicle on payment of an £80 fee. Most likely to be cherished are

(i) marks without a year identifier. These include marks issued in Great Britain before 1963, Northern Ireland marks and many sold at DVLA auctions (see opposite page).

(ii) marks which relate to a make or model of car, e.g. BMW 730L (on a BMW730iL), MGB 1Y (on an MGB), RR 1921 (on a 1921 Rolls-Royce), MC11 LAR (on a McLaren).

(iii) marks which spell a word or name, e.g. B1 NGO (Bingo), TOM 586S, 28 EVA, LOT 1A (on an auctioneer's car).

(iv) marks with the owner's initials. Many of these are DVLA 'Select' marks, see pages 42 and 43. (NOTE. 'Select' is a name

no longer used by the DVLA but it is retained here as a convenient description.)

Although it is illegal to space the characters on a number plate incorrectly (e.g. A S05AGE instead of AS05 AGE), some digits can be used to look like letters, in order to spell words or names, e.g. F570 KES to spell F Stokes, SU51 EPH to spell Susie P H.

The DVLA sells cherished registration marks which are newly created and have never before been issued (except those from the series BF 1 to BF 162 which were originally issued 1903/4). They are sold directly as 'Select' marks or are offered for sale at DVLA auctions and are chosen mainly from previously unfinished series of marks, or series which were never started. Some are reserved specially before their normal issue date because they are potentially attractive.

Personalised registrations are sold by the DVLA at auctions held several times a year (see page 45). Many of the marks on offer are without year identifier, some spell words and some are included in response to requests by members of the public. Many of these look like normally-issued old marks, but the newly created ones can be identified as they are listed in the Auction Sold Search section of the DVLA Registrations website (www.dvlaregistrations.direct.gov.uk/auction).

'SELECT' marks are generally less expensive than those sold at auctions. They can be ordered direct from the DVLA and are of two formats. Fuller details are given on pages 42 and 43.

Note that there are about thirty 'banned' three-letter combinations which are unavailable for either normal or select marks because they might cause offence, e.g. ASS, DAM, GOD, SOD, WOG.

CHERISHED MARKS

'SELECT' CURRENT-STYLE

A two-letter code consisting of any letters except I, Q, Z and FO, FU, MN and NF, followed by a year number, followed by three letters excluding I or Q.

During two months of the year (usually June and December for the forthcoming periods commencing September and March, see pages 6 and 7) the DVLA offers for sale any combination except those listed above, those with 'banned' three-letter groups (see page 41) or those withheld for sale by auction. It is sometimes impossible to distinguish these 'selects' from normally-issued marks.

Throughout the year the following may be purchased:- (a) two-letter code and last three letters ending the same (known as 'his and hers' pairs and favoured by married couples), e.g. C**T**08 J**AT**; (b) two-letter reserved by DVLA only for cherished marks (there are about fifty of these), such as AH, DR, GB, MR, OO, RU, VW, etc., e.g. **OO**05 SMW; (c) last three letters all the same, or spelling a word or name, e.g. VV11 **PPP**, AV14 **PET**.

All current-style marks beginning with J, T (except TF07, TJ07, TK07 and TN07), U or XG to XY, e.g. **J**O11 NYN, **U**F04 MRP, **XX**07 JAN are 'Select' and are not issued in the normal sequence.

'SELECT' OLD-STYLE

A prefix letter followed by a number of up to three digits followed by three letters. The prefix may be any letter except I, Q, U or Z.

'Select' old-style marks include

All prefixes (except those listed above): 1 to 20, e.g. S4 JCB, D**18** ECK.

From J to Y prefix (except Q and U):
round tens and hundreds, e.g. J80 JDG, P500 DJH.
doubles and trebles, e.g. P**66** BEE, M**777** CON.

From R to Y prefix* (except U): 21 to 31, 121, 123 and 321, e.g. T**29** POT, Y**31** LES, S**123** SAW.

K and M prefixes only: 155 (to resemble Kiss and Miss), e.g. K**155** DAN, M**155** AMY.

Last three letters are often the initials of the owner(s) and sometimes spell a word or name, e.g. R90 **PAT**, L999 **JET**.

Note. Some attractive marks of the above types are sold at DVLA auctions, e.g. F10 NAH (Fiona H), W1 NKS (Winks).

*Prefixes A to P will be available with these numbers at future dates.

The LTZ series, starting at LTZ 1001, has been specially allocated for New Bus for London (New Routemaster) buses

HOW TO OBTAIN A CHERISHED MARK

Cherished marks may be obtained
(a) from DVLA by bidding at a Personalised Registrations auction;
(b) from DVLA by applying direct ('Select' Registrations)
(c) from a dealer;
(d) from a private vendor.

(a) DVLA Auctions

Live Auctions are held five times a year at various localities throughout Great Britain. Bidding can be done in person, by telephone or on the internet. Information can be found on the DVLA Auction website (dvlaauction.co.uk) or by telephone 0300 123 0883 or by writing to DVLA Personalised Registrations, Swansea SA99 1DN. The website includes a list of all the registrations on offer at the next live auction. It is worth noting that the 'hammer price' at which the registration is sold is then subject to VAT, auctioneer's buyer's fee of 8% (plus VAT) and £80 assignment fee. Thus a registration bought for £500 would end up actually costing £728, and one bought for £1000 would cost £1376, etc.

Timed Auctions are held three times a year and bidding is normally done online. Details can be found at dvlaauction.co.uk.

(b) DVLA 'Select' Registrations

These can be either 'current-style' (e.g. PD15 TED) or 'old-style' (e.g. W99 YYX) and are described on pages 42 and 43. Available registrations can be found on the DVLA Personalised Registrations website (dvlaregistrations.direct.gov.uk).

(c) Dealers

Cherished marks of all kinds old and new can be bought from a dealer. Many reputable dealers have access to thousands of available marks which are listed in newspapers, e.g. Sunday Times, in motoring magazines and on the internet, e.g. regtransfers.co.uk who also publish a free full-colour magazine containing interesting articles and lists of their currently-available marks.

Make sure that any dealer you consult is a member of either (or both of) the Cherished Numbers Dealers Association (RMI Cherished Numbers Dealers Association, 201 Great Portland Street, London W1W 5AB. Tel: 0845 8399 205. Email: cnda@rmif.co.uk. Website: cnda.co.uk) or the Institute of Registration Agents and Dealers (MIRAD, PO Box 333, Southport PR9 7GW. Tel: 0300 030 1333. Email: enquiries@mirad.co.uk. Website: mirad.co.uk).

(d) Private Buying

Like most other commodities, registration marks can be traded on the open market. If buying privately, make quite sure that the mark is certain to be transferred to your ownership before you make any payment. Similarly, if you are selling a vehicle but wish to keep its cherished mark, **make sure that the mark has been transferred** (either to your replacement vehicle or to a retention certificate) **before you part with the vehicle.** See opposite page.

TRANSFERRING CHERISHED MARKS

To transfer a mark from one vehicle to another, go to the
website www.gov.uk/dvlaforms and download an application
form V317 which includes all the necessary information.
A transfer fee of £80 is payable when the application goes
ahead. If you are buying a cherished mark from a numbers
dealer, or are arranging the transfer through a car agent/
dealer, the paperwork is usually done for you.

RETENTION CERTIFICATES

A registration mark can be kept (retained) without putting it
on a vehicle. To retain a mark, go to the website
www.gov.uk/dvlaforms and download an application form
V317 or, to apply online, go to www.gov.uk/keep-registration-
number. On payment of a fee of £80 you will be issued with a
Retention Certificate V778 which is valid for ten years. The
mark can be transferred to a vehicle at any time or can be
retained for a further ten year period if desired.

REVIVING AN OLD MARK

A vehicle whose registration mark has never been included
in the DVLA records (a vehicle which has only an old-style
'log book' and has not been issued with a V5 registration
document or a V5C registration certificate) can still be
registered under its original mark if enough evidence can
be provided to show that the mark genuinely belongs to the
vehicle. Once a mark is registered in this way it must stay
with the original vehicle and cannot be transferred. Go to
www.gov.uk/dvlaforms and download form V765. You will
also need to complete form V55/5 which can be obtained from
DVLA Swansea, SA99 1AR (0300 790 6802).

AGE-RELATED MARKS

When an old vehicle is imported, or transferred from military or diplomatic to civilian use, or has its registration mark removed in a cherished transfer, or for some reason is being registered for the first time, a new mark is issued for it, normally 'age-related', i.e. a mark, taken from a previously unused series, which fits the age of the vehicle. Many veteran, vintage and classic cars carry these marks.

If the vehicle dates from 1963 or later, it is given a mark with the correct year-letter or year-number for its age, e.g. **V**139 LCC for a vehicle originally registered in January 2000. The three-letter codes on these marks formerly signified the place of issue but this is no longer the case. If the vehicle was manufactured earlier than 1963, it is given a mark from an old series without a year identifier.

Age-related series (pre-1963) so far are

Some EL, DEL and WFX marks	PSY 101 to YSY 999
	ASJ 101 to YSJ 998
SL 9737 to 9998	ASL 101 to YSL 998
DS 6574 to 9999	AAS 101 to RAS 998
SV 4001 to 9998	TAS 101 to YAS 998
BS 8000 onwards	UXG 101 to UXG 998
BF 4001 onwards	101 UXA to 998 UXY
ASV 101 to YSV 999	101 XUA to 998 XUY
CSU 101 to YSU 999	101 YUA to 998 YUY
BSK 101 to YSK 999	101 UYE to 998 UYY
GVS 101 to YVS 999	YVL 501 to 998
TYJ 101 to YYJ 999	YXG 501 to 998
KFF 101 to YFF 999	WXG 501 to 998
GFO 101 to YFO 999	

From July 2014, the 'reversed' series UYE to UYY have been issued to vehicles manufactured between 1953 and 1962. For vehicles manufactured from 1931 to 1952, the 'forward' series YVL, YXG and WXG have so far been allocated (as at June 2015).

Between 1983 and 1991 some old vehicles were given replacement marks with A, B or C suffix, e.g. ADC 214A on a 1955 Morris.

Current Age-related Series (as at June 2015)

Veteran vehicles (pre-1919): BS + four digits, e.g. BS 8630 on a 1903 Cadillac.

Vintage vehicles (1919-1930): BF + four digits, e.g. BF 5936 on a 1927 Ford.

Classic vehicles (1931-1952): WXG + three digits, e.g. WXG 919 on a 1938 MG.

Classic vehicles (1953-1962): three digits + UYE to UYY, e.g. 132 UYH on a 1958 Triumph.

Northern Ireland (pre-1975): IG + four digits, e.g. IG 4154 on a 1937 Morris.

The **IRISH REPUBLIC** in 1987 adopted its current system of registration marks. Until 2012 these were made up of the last two digits of the year, one or two letter code showing the place of issue, and up to six digits, normally with hyphens between the three groups of characters (e.g. 06-OY-2030 registered 2006 in Offaly). Plates are reflective white front and rear.

From 2013 a six-monthly variation of this system has been used. Registration marks begin with the last two digits of the year but with an added 1 for the period January to June, and 2 for the period July to December (e.g. 141-D-6333 registered in the first half of 2014 in Dublin).

Up to the end of 2013, the counties of Limerick, Tipperary and Waterford had two different codes (Limerick City L, Limerick County LK, Tipperary (North Riding) TN, Tipperary (South Riding) TS, Waterford City W, Waterford County WD). These still apply to any vehicle first registered before 2014 but new cars from January 2014 onwards are registered L, T and W respectively.

Trade plates in the Irish Republic are reflective green with white characters. The format is the reverse of the normal issue; the serial number is followed by the place of issue followed by the year of issue, e.g. 46-LH-93 (Louth 1993), 208-LM-14 (Leitrim 2014).

Trailers weighing more that 1524 Kg unladen carry extra plates with a separate series of codes.

Pre-1987 Marks

Before 1987 the Republic used the old-style pre-1963 U.K. system with a maximum of three letters and three digits, the last two letters signifying the place of issue (see pages 18 to 24). All marks included the letter I or the letter Z (or both). The plates were either black with white or silver characters, or reflective (white front, red rear) with black characters.

(Illustrations on page 52)

Current county codes are:-

C   Cork
CE   Clare
CN   Cavan
CW   Carlow
D   Dublin
DL   Donegal
G   Galway
KE   Kildare
KK   Kilkenny
KY   Kerry
L   Limerick
LD   Longford
LH   Louth
LM   Leitrim
LS   Laois
MH   Meath
MN   Monaghan
MO   Mayo
OY   Offaly
RN   Roscommon
SO   Sligo
T   Tipperary
W   Waterford
WH   Westmeath
WW   Wicklow
WX   Wexford

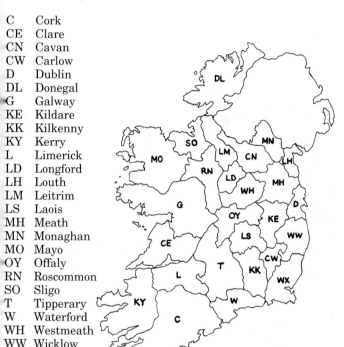

ZV followed by three to five digits on black plates is used for vehicles over 30 years of age if the old-style format is preferred. **ZZ** followed by five digits is used for temporary import/export registrations.

(Illustrations on page 52)

Cork, 2014 (July-December)   Longford, 2008

Dublin, 1986   Old-style mark for vehicle over 30 years old

Westmeath, 1966   Trade plate, Waterford, 2013

Number plates used on vehicles registered in the U.K. can include, at the left-hand end, a band depicting the European Union (EU) emblem with the letters GB below the emblem. This is usually recognised internationally as denoting U.K. origin and a GB oval (see pages 65 to 67) is not needed when travelling in EU countries.

The EU band is also shown on most of the number plates issued in the other 27 member countries of the Union (Austria, Belgium, Bulgaria, Croatia, Cyprus, Czech Republic, Denmark, Estonia, Finland, France, Germany, Greece, Hungary, Ireland, Italy, Latvia, Lithuania, Luxembourg, Malta, Netherlands, Poland, Portugal, Romania, Slovakia, Slovenia, Spain and Sweden). The EU emblem consists of a circle of twelve gold stars.

The U.K. Government also permits the display of 'national' emblems and letters in place of the EU band. These depict the Union flag (Union Jack) with letters GB, cross of St George with letters ENG, Scottish saltire (X cross) with letters SCO or Welsh red dragon with letters CYM (short for Cymru, the Welsh name for Wales). These, however, are not internationally recognised and a GB oval plate should also be displayed when travelling abroad.

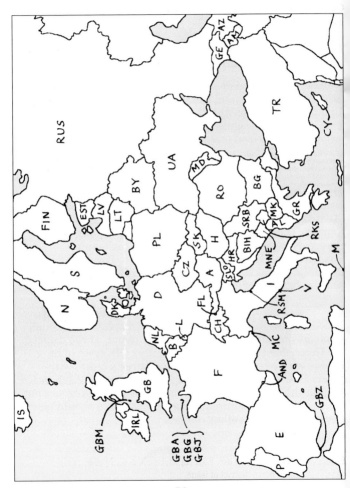

Characters (capital letters or digits) on number plates are black on a white background unless otherwise stated.

The International Identification Code is shown in brackets after the country's name.

Member countries of the European Union are marked :**EU**: . Their number plates normally have a blue band on the left with the EU logo (a circle of 12 golden stars) above the international code (see page 53).

Descriptions refer to normal issue registrations for private cars from left to right of number plate. In most countries there are many variations of these patterns for special types of vehicles, e.g. different colouring, different lettering, varied order of letters and digits, etc. Each country has its own rules, so variations can apply to personalised numbers, older vehicles, diplomatic cars, export vehicles, hire cars, etc., etc.

ALBANIA (AL) Blue band on left with double-headed eagle above AL. Two letters, security hologram, three digits, two letters.

ANDORRA (AND) Coat of arms on left and PRINCIPAT D'ANDORRA at bottom. One letter, four digits.

ARMENIA (AM) National flag on left above AM. Two or three digits, two letters, two or three digits (maximum 7 characters). First two digits show province of issue.

AUSTRIA (A) :EU: Two red lines along top, two red lines along bottom. One or two letters, federal state emblem, up to six characters. First letter(s) denote(s) place of issue, e.g. S=Salzburg.

AZERBAIJAN (AZ) National flag above AZ. Two digits, hyphen, two letters, hyphen, three digits. First two digits show area of issue.

BELARUS (BY) Flag top left. Four digits, two letters, hyphen, one digit. Last digit shows district of issue.

Albania

Andorra

Armenia

Austria

Azerbaijan

Belarus

Belgium

Bosnia & Herzegovina

Bulgaria

Croatia

Cyprus

Czech Republic

BELGIUM (B) :EU: Red characters on white background. One digit, hyphen, three letters, hyphen, three digits.

BOSNIA & HERZEGOVINA (BIH). Blue band with BIH on left. One letter, two digits, hyphen, one letter, hyphen, three digits.

BULGARIA (BG) :EU: One or two letters, space, four digits, two letters. First letter(s) denote(s) province of issue.

CROATIA (HR) :EU: Red and blue lines along top and bottom. Two letters, Croatian coat of arms, three or four digits, hyphen, one or two letters. First two letters denote region of issue. (New style with EU band to be introduced 2015.)

CYPRUS (CY) :EU: Three letters, up to three digits. Month and year of first registration are shown as small numbers in central space.

CZECH REPUBLIC (CZ) :EU: One digit, one letter, one character (digit or letter), inspection seals, four digits. The first (or only) letter denotes place of issue.

DENMARK (DK) :EU: Red border. Optional blue Euro band on left. Two letters, five digits.

ESTONIA (EST) :EU: Three digits, three letters. (Pre-2013 the first letter denoted region of issue.)

FINLAND (FIN) :EU: Three letters, hyphen, three digits.

FRANCE (F) :EU: Two letters, three digits, two letters. Blue band on right shows regional code at bottom with (sometimes) regional logo above.

GEORGIA (GE) Blue band on left with national flag above GE. Two letters, hyphen, three digits, hyphen, two letters.

GERMANY (D) :EU: One, two or three letters (denoting place of issue), two seal stickers, one or two letters, up to four digits (maximum total of eight characters).

Denmark

Estonia

Finland

France

Georgia

Germany

Greece

Hungary

Iceland

Italy

Kosovo

Latvia

GIBRALTAR (GBZ) :EU: White front, yellow rear. Letter G, four digits, letter.

GREECE (GR) :EU: Three letters, hyphen, four digits. The first two letters denote district of issue.

HUNGARY (H) :EU: Three letters, hyphen, three digits.

ICELAND (IS) Iceland flag top left. Blue characters on a white background. Two letters, inspection sticker, three characters (either three digits or one letter and two digits).

ITALY (I) :EU: Two letters, small republic seal, three digits, two letters. Optional blue band on right shows place of issue.

KOSOVO (RKS) Blue band on left with RKS. Two digits, Kosovan coat of arms, three digits, hyphen, two letters. The first two digits denote district of issue.

LATVIA (LV) :EU: Two letters, hyphen, up to four digits.

LIECHTENSTEIN (FL) White characters on black background. FL, coat of arms of Liechtenstein, up to five digits.

LITHUANIA (LT) :EU: Three letters, inspection sticker, three digits.

LUXEMBOURG (L) :EU: Black characters on yellow background. Two letters, four digits (or up to five digits without letters).

MACEDONIA (MK) Blue band on left with MK. Two letters, red square with first two and last two letters in Cyrillic print, four digits, two letters. First two letters denote region of issue.

MALTA (M) :EU: Three letters, three digits.

FL · 22655

Liechtenstein

BEM · 113

Lithuania

JK 1903

Luxembourg

GV 0735 AB

Macedonia

JAJ · 236

Malta

CT AL 569 ·

Moldova

Y078

Monaco

CT · AC763

Montenegro

35-GNH-4

Netherlands

KH 53523

Norway

TST · 29KT

Poland

09 · AE · 12 05/06

Portugal

MOLDOVA (MD) Blue band with national emblem above MD. Two letters (or single C or K), two letters, three digits. First pair of letters (or single C or K) denotes place of issue. (New style being introduced 2015: blue band with national flag above MD, German-style characters.)

MONACO (MC) Coat of arms on left. Blue characters on white background. PRINCIPAUTÉ DE MONACO along bottom. Four digits/letters.

MONTENEGRO (MNE) Blue band on left with MNE. Two letters, coat of arms, two letters, three digits. First two letters denote place of issue.

NETHERLANDS (NL) :EU: Yellow background. Six characters of three groups (letter groups or digit groups of one, two or three characters) separated by hyphens.

NORWAY (N) Blue band with Norwegian flag. Two letters, four or five digits. The letters denote the place of issue.

POLAND (PL) :EU: Two or three letters, four or five characters (maximum total of seven characters). First group of letters denotes place of issue.

PORTUGAL (P) :EU: Two digits, hyphen, two letters, hyphen, two digits.

ROMANIA (RO) :EU: Two letters (or single letter B), two digits (or three digits with single B), three letters. First two letters (or single B for Bucharest) denote county of issue.

RUSSIA (RUS) One letter, three larger digits, two letters. In panel on right, above RUS and Russian flag, number denoting place of issue.

SAN MARINO (RSM) Coat of arms on left above REPUBBLICA DI SAN MARINO. Five blue characters on a white background. One letter, four digits (or no letters and five digits).

Romania

Russia

San Marino

Serbia

Slovakia

Slovenia

Spain

Sweden

Switzerland

Turkey

Ukraine

Vatican City

SERBIA (SRB) Blue band on left with SRB. Two letters, coat of arms, three digits, dot, two letters. First two letters denote region of issue. Under coat of arms is region code in Cyrillic lettering.

SLOVAKIA (SK) :EU: Two letters, coat of arms, three digits, two letters. First two letters denote district of issue.

SLOVENIA (SLO) :EU: Green border. Two letters (region of issue), coat of arms (town of issue), two characters, hyphen, three characters.

SPAIN (E) :EU: Four digits, three letters.

SWEDEN (S) :EU: Three letters, three digits

SWITZERLAND (CH) Two letters (regional code), up to six digits. Rear plates have Swiss coat of arms (left end) and region (canton) coat of arms (right end).

TURKEY (TR) Blue band on left with TR. Two digits, one, two or three letters, up to five digits (maximum eight characters). First two digits show province of issue

UKRAINE (UA) Band on left has emblem on blue background above UA on yellow background (From 2015, blue band on left with national flag above UA.) Two letters, four digits, two letters. First two letters denote region of issue.

VATICAN CITY (V) SCV or CV, up to five digits.

UNITED STATES OF AMERICA (USA) Plates are smaller than those normally used in the UK. Each of the fifty states has its own system of registration and its own types and colours of plate, many with illustrations commemorating events, charities, etc. The state name is included on the plate.

Left: Qatar. Maroon serrated band on left (as in Qatari flag) with QATAR depicted vertically. Right: Abu Dhabi (UAE). Red panel with white number. Many plates (but not all) have U.A.E. A.D. at bottom.

Left: Dubai (UAE). Letter plus up to five digits. Right: Saudi Arabia. Four digits and three letters (Arabic script equivalent on top line). Band on right KSA (Kingdom of Saudi Arabia) below national emblem (palm tree surmounting two crossed swords).

Left: Kuwait. One or two digits, hyphen, up to five digits. Shorter plates have first digit, or group of digits, above second group, and band on left with KUWAIT depicted vertically. Right: Bahrain. National flag on left of number.

64

INTERNATIONAL CODES

An international code is displayed either on an oval plate or sticker (usually on the back of the vehicle), or on a band as part of the number plate, to identify the country of origin when travelling abroad.

A	Austria	**CDN**	Canada
AFG	Afghanistan	**CH**	Switzerland
AL	Albania	**CI**	Côte d'Ivoire
AM	Armenia	**CL**	Sri Lanka
AND	Andorra	**CO**	Colombia
AUS	Australia	**CR**	Costa Rica
AZ	Azerbaijan	**CY**	Cyprus
		CZ	Czech Republic
B	Belgium		
BD	Bangladesh	**D**	Germany
BDS	Barbados	**DK**	Denmark
BF	Burkina Faso	**DOM**	Dominican Republic
BG	Bulgaria	**DY**	Benin
BIH	Bosnia & Herzegovina	**DZ**	Algeria
BOL	Bolivia		
BR	Brazil	**E**	Spain
BRN	Bahrain	**EAK**	Kenya
BRU	Brunei	**EAT**	Tanzania (Tanganyika)
BS	Bahamas	**EAU**	Uganda
BUR	Myanmar	**EAZ**	Tanzania (Zanzibar)
BVI	British Virgin Islands	**EC**	Ecuador
BW	Botswana	**ER**	Eritrea
BY	Belarus	**ES**	El Salvador
BZ	Belize	**EST**	Estonia
		ET	Egypt
C	Cuba	**ETH**	Ethiopia
CAM	Cameroon		
CD	Corps Diplomatique	**F**	France
	(Used on some foreign	**FIN**	Finland
	diplomatic cars)	**FJI**	Fiji

INTERNATIONAL CODES

FL	Liechtenstein	**L**	Luxembourg
FO	Faroe Islands	**LAO**	Laos
FSM	Micronesia	**LAR**	Libya
		LB	Liberia
G	Gabon	**LS**	Lesotho
GB	United Kingdom	**LT**	Lithuania
GBA	Alderney	**LV**	Latvia
GBG	Guernsey		
GBJ	Jersey	**M**	Malta
GBM	Isle of Man	**MA**	Morocco
GBZ	Gibraltar	**MAL**	Malaysia
GCA	Guatemala	**MC**	Monaco
GE	Georgia	**MD**	Moldova
GH	Ghana	**MEX**	Mexico
GR	Greece	**MGL**	Mongolia
GUY	Guyana	**MK**	Macedonia
		MNE	Montenegro
H	Hungary	**MOC**	Mozambique
HK	Hong Kong	**MS**	Mauritius
HKJ	Jordan	**MW**	Malawi
HR	Croatia		
		N	Norway
I	Italy	**NA**	Netherlands Antilles
IL	Israel	**NAM**	Namibia
IND	India	**NAU**	Nauru
IR	Iran	**NEP**	Nepal
IRL	Ireland	**NGR**	Nigeria
IRQ	Iraq	**NIC**	Nicaragua
IS	Iceland	**NL**	Netherlands
		NZ	New Zealand
J	Japan		
JA	Jamaica	**P**	Portugal
		PA	Panama
KH	Cambodia	**PE**	Peru
KS	Kyrgyzstan	**PK**	Pakistan
KSA	Saudi Arabia	**PL**	Poland
KWT	Kuwait	**PNG**	Papua New Guinea
KZ	Kazakhstan	**PY**	Paraguay

Q	Qatar	**SYR**	Syria
RA	Argentina	**T**	Thailand
RC	Taiwan	**TCH**	Chad
RCA	Central African Republic	**TG**	Togo
RCB	Congo (Republic)	**TJ**	Tajikistan
RCH	Chile	**TM**	Turkmenistan
RG	Guinea	**TN**	Tunisia
RH	Haiti	**TR**	Turkey
RI	Indonesia	**TT**	Trinidad & Tobago
RIM	Mauritania		
RKS	Kosovo	**UA**	Ukraine
RL	Lebanon	**UAE**	United Arab Emirates
RM	Madagascar	**USA**	United States of America
RMM	Mali	**UY**	Uruguay
RN	Niger	**UZ**	Uzbekistan
RO	Romania		
ROK	South Korea	**V**	Vatican
RP	Philippines	**VN**	Vietnam
RSM	San Marino		
RU	Burundi	**WAG**	Gambia
RUS	Russia	**WAL**	Sierra Leone
RWA	Rwanda	**WD**	Dominica
		WG	Grenada
S	Sweden	**WL**	St Lucia
SD	Swaziland	**WS**	Samoa
SGP	Singapore	**WV**	St Vincent & Grenadines
SK	Slovakia		
SLO	Slovenia	**YAR**	Yemen
SME	Suriname	**YV**	Venezuela
SN	Senegal		
SO	Somalia	**Z**	Zambia
SRB	Serbia	**ZA**	South Africa
SUD	Sudan	**ZRE**	Congo (Dem. Republic)
SY	Seychelles	**ZW**	Zimbabwe

CURRENT-STYLE. Try to spot a **current-style** mark from each of the forty-one areas. For codes, see pages 8 to 13. If you can't find a certain code, the mark is probably cherished so could be entered on page 75.

Where issued	Reg. Mark	When/where seen
Aberdeen		
Bangor		
Birmingham		
Bournemouth		
Brighton		
Bristol		
Cardiff		
Carlisle		
Chelmsford		
Chester		
Dundee		
Edinburgh		
Exeter		
Glasgow		
Hull		
Inverness		
Ipswich		
Isle of Wight		
Leeds		

Where issued	Reg. Mark	When/where seen
Lincoln		
London N/West		
London S/East		
London S/West		
Luton (2001-7)		
Maidstone		
Manchester		
Middlesbrough		
Newcastle		
Northampton		
Norwich		
Nottingham		
Oxford		
Peterborough		
Portsmouth		
Preston		
Reading		
Sheffield		
Shrewsbury		
Swansea		
Truro		
Worcester		
XA to XF		

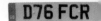

OLD-STYLE PREFIX marks (issued 1983 to 2001). Try to spot marks with different prefixes (see pages 14 to 24). Don't count any with numbers 1 to 20 (see page 43) as these are 'Select' marks.

Reg. mark	Where issued	When/where seen
A		
B		
C		
D		
E		
F		
G		
H		
J		
K		
L		
M		
N		
P		
Q		
R		
S		
T		
V		
W		
X		
Y		

OLD-STYLE SUFFIX marks (issued 1963 to 1983) are now becoming quite rare, especially the earlier ones. See if you can spot one of each. See pages 14 to 24.

Reg. mark	Where issued	When/where seen
A		
B		
C		
D		
E		
F		
G		
H		
J		
K		
L		
M		
N		
P		
R		
S		
T		
V		
W		
X		
Y		

JE 4|5 **EKZ 3|36**

OLD-STYLE WITHOUT YEAR LETTERS (before 1963/5).

Usually classic, vintage or veteran vehicles with black number plates. Classic car rallies are good places to spot them. Look out, too, for Replacements (new marks on old vehicles, see pages 48 and 49). Codes are on pages 18 to 24.

Reg. mark	Where issued	When/where seen

NORTHERN IRELAND. Usually three letters (including I or Z) followed by up to four digits. See page 26.

Reg. mark	Where issued	When/where seen

IRISH REPUBLIC. See pages 50 to 52.   **02-KE-6|65**

Reg. mark	Where issued	When/where seen

OFFSHORE ISLANDS. Isle of Man, Jersey, Guernsey
Alderney, Scilly Isles. See pages 28 to 30.

Reg. mark	Where issued	When/where seen

OTHER COUNTRIES. See pages 55 to 67.

Reg. mark	Country	When/where seen

TRADE PLATES. Red numbers, or numbers and letters, on a white background (see page 27). Spot these at car dealers and garages. For codes, see pages 18 to 24.

Reg. mark	Where issued	When/where seen

MILITARY. Quite often seen on the roads, and especially near navy, air force and army bases or in military museums. See pages 31 and 32.

Reg. mark	Vehicle type	When/where seen

DIPLOMATIC. Most easily spotted in London. See pages 33 to 37.

Reg. mark	Make of car	When/where seen

CHERISHED MARKS. Old-style marks on new cars, <u>or</u>
letters which spell words or names, <u>or</u> number plates with initials
of famous people or people you know, <u>or</u> certain kinds of new-style
marks, etc. See pages 40 to 43.

Reg. mark	Make of vehicle	When/where seen

The Driver and Vehicle Licensing Centre with its prominent
16-storey office block is situated at Morriston on the outskirts of
Swansea. It was conceived by the government in 1965 and opened
in 1967 to centralise and computerise the driver and vehicle records
formerly held by councils in Great Britain (England, Wales and
Scotland). It became fully operational in 1974. The Centre has
been run since 1990 as the DVLA, an agency of the Department
for Transport (DfT). Since 2014 it has also become responsible for
records formerly held by DVA Northern Ireland.

The DVLA currently holds details of over 45 million licensed drivers
and over 37 million licensed vehicles. In addition to its principal task
of maintaining and updating these records and issuing licences and
registration documents, it collects and enforces vehicle excise duty
and provides data for the police and other agencies.

Information about vehicles recorded on the DVLA database can
be found on www.vehicleenquiry.service.gov.uk by entering the
registration mark and the make of vehicle (if the make is unknown it
can be found by first looking on a vehicle checking website). Details
include year of manufacture, date of first registration, colour, type of
body, engine cylinder capacity, amount of tax payable and whether
the vehicle is currently taxed, etc. The names or addresses of vehicle
owners or keepers are not released by the DVLA except in special
circumstances, e.g. tracing owners of abandoned vehicles, owners of
vehicles involved in accidents, or crimes such as fraud.

EUROPLATE

Europlate (The European Registration Plate Association) was formed in 1972 and now has around 330 members in 32 countries. It welcomes all those interested in registration marks and plates worldwide. The Association holds a convention every two years and publishes a quarterly newsletter (see below), illustrated throughout with several pages in full colour. Membership costs £19.00 a year (for printed newsletter) or £14.00 (for pdf version). Details can be obtained from Europlate, Plas Rheged, 20 Marden Grove, Taunton TA1 2RT, or from the website www.europlate.org.uk

Membership also gives unlimited access to the website which incorporates a full colour edition of 'Registration Plates of the World' (now out of print in book form). This is a compendium of detailed information covering every country, describing and illustrating current and earlier registration series with historical notes.

1903 AND ALL THAT

A quarterly newsletter which deals with all aspects of vehicle registrations both current and historical. For a sample copy and subscription details please send a large stamped (for a large letter over 100 grams) addressed envelope to John Harrison, 175 Hillyfields, Loughton IG10 2PW.

REGISTRATION NUMBERS CLUB

The Registration Numbers Club (RNC), founded in January 1977 by a group of enthusiasts in the North of England, has a membership of over 400 and welcomes all cherished number enthusiasts and owners.The Club publishes a full-colour quarterly magazine (see left) and organizes an annual rally. Details of membership can be obtained from Registration Numbers Club, 39 Winding Way, Leeds LS17 7RG.
Website:www.theRNC.co.uk

CAR NUMBERS – THEN AND NOW

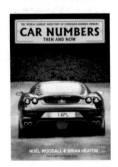

by Noël Woodall and Brian Heaton. The latest edition of this famous directory of cherished numbers and their owners. Contains details of many thousands of owners, and all 'number 1' registrations sold by DVLA (up to the time of publication) with their auction prices. Illustrated with over 200 photos, many in colour, the book also includes a reprint of the text of Noël's first hardback book 'Who's Who' (1966) which has long been out of print but is still regularly requested by enthusiasts. A5, 896 pages, hard cover. Published 2008. £45.00
(ISBN 9780952071655).

A HISTORY OF MOTOR VEHICLE REGISTRATION
THE UNITED KINGDOM (Third edition)
by L H Newall with revisions edited by John Harrison

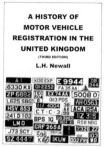

Les Newall spent a lifetime researching the history of the
UK registration system and this book is the product of his
research. He tells the story of the development of registration
marks from their introduction in 1903 and gives detailed
information about 'ordinary' marks, trade plates, diplomatic
marks, military registrations and the British cherished number system.

A large part of the book is taken up with a council-by-council
survey which includes dates of issue of all known pre-1964
two-letter and three-letter marks. For those owners and
enthusiasts wishing to find out more about the origins of particular marks, this book is invaluable.

The book features eight pages of photographs depicting over
fifty vehicles bearing the various types of registration mark
described in the text. It also includes an index and a chapter
explaining how the current registration system introduced in
2001 has actually worked out in practice.

A5, vi + 320 pages. Laminated card cover. Published 2008,
reprinted 2012. Price £16.95. (ISBN 9781872686325).

ACKNOWLEDGMENTS AND PICTURE CREDITS

The author wishes to acknowledge his indebtedness to Brian Heaton and the late Noël Woodall for information from their book 'Where's It From? When Was It Issued?' and to many city, town and county councils for details of their official cars.

Thanks also to the following for permission to use their photographs (t=top, b=bottom, l=left, r=right):-

contributors to nice-reg.co.uk: David Harold (39br), Finlay C (37r), Raffles (2ml, 36l, 39bl), Robert Clark (2mr, 36r), and SMT-Photos (49br);

contributors to plateshack.com (Y2K): Mike Sells (58 Greece, 60 Montenegro, 63 all), Dr Sergio Da Camera (front cover 222D952, 56 Azerbaijan, Belgium, Bosnia & Herzegovina, 62 San Marino), Andrew Osborne (58 Iceland), John O Perez (56 Albania, Croatia, 58 Denmark, 62 Turkey) and Jochen M Voelsch (62 Vatican);

contributors to platesmania.com: astonkas (12r), GTR Jacko (2tl);

and to Brendan Aanes (64mr), Barrak Al-Sarraf (64bl), Giorgi Balakhadze (58 Georgia), Dermot Comerford (52ml, mr, br), DVLA (76), europlates.eu (59, 60 Macedonia), Michael J Heavey (52tr), Horsepower Cars Inverness (12l), Krokodyl (58 Finland), Chris Lemons (44), licenseplatemania.com (front cover MAN-336), licenseplatesintheworld.com (front cover and 56 Andorra), licenseplatespics.com (64tr, ml), Donald MacFarlane (27tl), Midlothian Council (39tl), Ministry of Defence (32tr), Noel Deasy Cars Ltd (52tl), olavsplates.com (29ml, 60 Moldova), Royal Borough of Windsor and Maidenhead (39tr), Cedric Sabine via Francoplaque (56 Armenia), Ivan Thornley (27br), Rosta Uhlar (29tr), Veteran Car Sales (49tl), youreuropemap.com (54, adapted from the original) and Zack's Motor Photos (49tr).

Inclusion of registration ET 1 (page 39) by kind permission of Rotherham Metropolitan Borough Council.